ORDER MY STEPS

ORDER MY STEPS

A True Story of Purpose and Resilience from Childhood through Adolescence

ERIC PIERRE ISAACS

Editor - Shelly Rotte

PIEZILLIE
Publishing Co.

Piezillie Publishing Co.

Order My Steps: A True Story of Purpose and Resilience from Childhood through Adolescence

Copyright © 2020 by ERIC PIERRE ISAACS

First Printing, 2020

Library of Congress Cataloging-in-Publication Data

Piezillie Publishing Company, LLC
Cincinnati, OH 45239
piezilliepublishing@gmail.com

ISBN: 978-1-7363462-0-4 (Paperback)
      978-1-7363462-1-1 (E-book)

PIEZILLIE
Publishing Co.

Printed in the United States of America
Edited by Shelly Rotte
Illustrated by Davide Dart Rota, Olabode S. Ajiboye, and Eric Pierre Isaacs
Cover Design by Eric Pierre Isaacs, Canva.com
Interior Layout and Design by Eric Pierre Isaacs

Dedicated to my Ancestors and
Descendants

Contents

Prologue

Order my steps in Your Word, dear Lord
Lead me, guide me every day
Send your anointing, Father, I pray
Order my steps in Your Word

Chapter 1

The Awakening

"Dear brothers and sisters, when troubles come your way, consider it an opportunity for great joy. For you know that when your faith is tested, your endurance has a chance to grow." **James 1:2-3**

My first memory in life is being stung by a bee on a hot summer day. The sun was shining bright, and the birds were chirping. I was playing outside in the neighborhood that I lived in at the time. I was exploring and discovering Nature as every boy should, but Mother Nature does demand her respect.

Somehow, my adventurous escapade led me into aggravating and disturbing a group of nearby bees. I first felt a tickle on my ear, but that did not alert me of the danger that I was in. Before I realized it, one of the bees had perched on my ear and stung me in the upper left lobe. The experience is welded in my memory because of the extreme pain associated with it. It was a wasp, but as a kid, it didn't matter to me. All I knew was that *some flying insect called a bee had attacked me for no understandable reason.* I ran home crying and in tears in search of comfort. My Mom came outside, assured me that everything was going to be okay, and took the stinger out of my ear. She then nursed my wound and hurt feelings enough for me to live on. I recovered emotionally minutes later, but the experience made me leery of bees moving forward.

Next, I remember riding my blue battery-powered motorcycle back and forth on the sidewalk. I consciously steered clear of the territory that was now marked by the bees after the attack. Little did I know that even then, God was ordering my steps. He used these bees to teach me a valuable life lesson.

I believe that God was showing me early on during childhood that living in this world was going to include feeling some pain, but there would also be a joy that follows that pain. I remember feeling the overwhelming joy in my body from simply returning to play after the wrath of being stung. Surely and thankfully, there would be calm after the storm.

No human could ever possess the infinite knowledge, understanding, and wisdom of God. Our understanding is mere crumbs on His plate. However, I am what I am by the grace of God, and I am made in His image. Upon reflection of my life's events, one thing is crystal clear to me; God has ordered every single step throughout my life's journey. The man I am today is His creation and design, and without Him, I am absolutely nothing.

Tera Lee and Eric Pierre Isaacs

Chapter 2

Footprints

"A joyful heart is a good medicine, but a crushed spirit dries up the bones." **Proverbs 17:22**

My Dad's parents were named Marion Neblett and Arthur Isaacs. From their union came eleven children. I never got a chance to meet my paternal grandmother. This was because she had already passed away before I was born. Her parents were Eudora Gee and Stewart Neblett. Eudora, my great grandmother, passed away at the age of 22 due to complications from having children so young and consecutively. From the stories I've heard, her parents, George and Ida Washington were both upset with my great grandfather Stewart for rushing Eudora to have so many children. They felt that he did not give her enough time to recover in between her pregnancies. As a result, they distanced themselves from the other side of my family upon her death. My grandmother Marian had an older brother, Nick Neblett Jr., who was an original Tuskegee Airman. He lived well into his old age, and I was able to meet and get to know him while he was living. Even at an old age, he was still very mentally sharp for an older man.

I have vague memories of when I was younger and getting a chance to spend some time with my grandfather Arthur Isaacs. His parents, who are my great grandparents, were Arthur Isaac and Caroline Williams. My Dad would occasionally take me over to my grandfather's house to visit him. He was introduced to me as my grandpa Ike. He was married to a woman named Martha, whom we fondly referred to as Grandma Martha. By this time, my granddad was in a wheelchair and needed constant assistance from my Grandma Martha to perform basic household activities. I remember Grandma Martha having to help my grandfather eat and use the restroom. Their house had a distinctive smell, and it reminded me of a stale or mildew type of odor. It wasn't stinky, but the remnants of it remain in my nostrils. I'm pretty sure it was a mothball smell, but as a kid, I associated the smell with older folks.

I have two distinct memories of my paternal grandfather. I remember going to visit him, and he would be perched in his wheelchair in front of the television watching wrestling. I remember he would mimic flexing his muscles above his head just like "The Narcissist" Lex Luger. I would imitate him and emulate those motions as well. It always made me feel strong, and my grandpa would chuckle to see me following his lead. This started my love and fascination with professional wrestling.

The second memory I have of him was at his funeral. A multitude of people showed up for the service, as most of the pews were occupied. My grandfather was laid to rest in a big grey church, and I remember seeing my Dad weep and grieve. This memory stands out because it was the first time I saw him in such a vulnerable state. Before that, I saw my Dad as being untouchable and larger than life. This was also my first encounter with death, but I was much too young to fully understand that my grandfather was not returning to his earthly form. I didn't weep for him because we weren't extremely close. However, I remember the impact it had on me as a kid. I was emotionally stable during the ceremony but deeply saddened from observing others in their time of bereavement. What I did understand, however, was that I no longer would have a living grandfather on either side of my family.

My Mom's parents were named Lawrence Albert Turley and Sara Lee Turley. By trade, my Grandpa was a well-renowned jeweler in the city of Cincinnati. He was a model as well. His nick-name was Love, and he was known for creating unique pieces of jewelry. Grandpa never made the same piece of jewelry twice. He had an excellent sense of style, fashion, and he was also a model. At a young age, I discovered my love and ability to draw, and I was told that the artistic trait was passed down from my Grandpa. He died just one year before I was born in 1983; however, through art, I feel as if we have always been connected in some way. My grandfather was married to my grandmother, and together, they had two children: my mother and Uncle Topper, respectively. My Grandma Sarah had Debbie prior to marrying my Grandpa, but he raised Debbie as his own. Both of my grandparents each had a child from outside relationships. My Grandpa had a daughter named Natalie and my Grandma Sarah had a son by the name of Mark.

My Grandma Sarah was the only grandparent I have ever really got to know. She made a major impact on my life during my childhood. I believe God used her to show me the true meaning of unconditional love. She nurtured me with a love so pure that words cannot fully express it. The grandchildren could do no wrong in the eyes of my Grandma Sarah. My grandfather urged my grandmother to start her own business earlier on in their relationship. She listened, went to cosmetology school, and then opened her Hair Salon. Styling hair became a family legacy passed down to my mother, sister, and other family members as well.

My Grandmother is the main character in one of my favorite stories from childhood. Ever since I was young, I enjoyed swimming. My sister Tera taught me how to swim at the pool in the complex where my grandmother lived. The neighborhood that I grew up in also had a pool at the time. During the summers, Ricardo and I would swim all day long every time we were allowed to go to the neighborhood pool. You needed to be supervised at the pool if you were younger than 13. However, my brother and I had become familiar with the lifeguards, so they would let us swim. I think they felt bad for us because we simply wanted to swim and were excellent young swimmers already. Their way of getting around the rule was by training us to become junior lifeguards. They taught us how to dive, how to rescue, and formal swim techniques. I am grateful for their compassion and supervision. They also gave me a pair of flippers, which became a prized possession of mine. The flippers made me extremely fast and swift in the water.

One day after returning from swimming, I had mistakenly left or dropped one of my slippers downstairs in the basement. My step-father, Creester, had a rule that if the kids left any item outside of their rooms, then it was subject to be thrown away. I always felt like it was cruel and unusual punishment. When I returned to the basement, I noticed the flipper on the ground and Creester then moving towards it to collect it. I darted in to retrieve the flipper, but Creester had already picked it up. I pleaded and begged him to return the flipper to me. He refused to and insisted on taking it. Hence, I made one last desperate attempt and lunged for the flipper. Creester grabbed the arm I was reaching for the flipper with and forcefully threw me down the hallway. My arm hit against the corner of the wall and then began to bleed. I began to sob, and I was distraught that he had injured me and taken my possession. It was enough to force that I still have a scar from that incident today. I pleaded with my Mom to intervene, but she stood by my Stepdad's decision.

I did not call the Cincinnati Police, Child Protective Services, or the National Guard, but I did call my Grandma Sarah. I told her what happened, and she comforted me and assured me that everything was going to be okay. In what seemed like a very short time, I heard a large screeching sound right outside my basement window. I peeked out the window and realized that it was my grandmother's Cadillac. I immediately panicked because my Mom and Stepdad had no idea what I had told my Grandmother. All I could think to do was unlock the basement door for them and then hide in the closet adjacent to it. I cracked the door open just enough for me to peek through the small opening to get a glimpse of the drama that was about to unfold. I was scared, and my heart was pounding in my chest as I anticipated the confrontation. The next thing I know, my grandma had busted the door open, with her fancy sunglasses on and her purse hanging from her forearm. She charged straight up the stairs, and Uncle Topper, cousin Tamaine, and cousin Twan followed behind. The men had bats, chains, and two by fours in their arms as they marched forward. I stayed in the closet because the situation had escalated, and I could hear what was happening on the steps above my head.

My Mother became aware of the oncoming onslaught and stopped my Grandma Sarah at the top of the steps. They exchanged some heated words, and my mother pleaded with my grandmother to de-escalate the situation. My Grandma agreed to not order the small mob to attack Creester, but she was very much insistent on dealing with the issue. The confrontation lasted for several minutes. After the heated exchange, my grandmother had made her point clear and was satisfied with leaving. I remember seeing and hearing her as she walked out the door proclaiming as she pointed her finger in the air, "He ain't going to hit MINE!" My Mom was upset with me, but I loved my Grandma Sarah for coming to my rescue. She defended me when I had nowhere else to turn. This was a story that she made sure I never forgot, as we laughed about it years later. The flipper was eventually returned, and from that time forward, anytime I got in trouble Creester put me on punishment. That was a consequence that I could accept from him, especially since he wasn't my real Dad.

Marian Neblett

Arthur Isaacs

Sarah Lee Turley and Lawrence Albert Turley

Chapter 3

Blood is Thicker than Water

"Train up a child in the way he should go: and when he is old, he will not depart from it." **Proverbs 22:6**

I was born on December 6, 1983, in Cincinnati, Ohio, at Christ Hospital. The doctor that delivered me was named Jan Smoke. My birth parents were Teresa Terry Turley and Eric James Isaacs. Life has shown me that I am a healthy mix of both my parents and their personalities. I have three other siblings from this union, and one other half-sister from my Dad, and a previous relationship, before my Mom. I am the oldest boy of four children. Although I am not directly named after my Dad, I was always acknowledged as Little Eric and His Junior. I have two younger twin brothers named Rico Alonzo Isaacs and Ricardo Alfonso Isaacs, respectively. I am three years older than my brothers and six years younger than my sister Tera.

Erica J. Holloman is the name of my half-sister from my Dad's relationship previous to my Mom. I knew of my sister Erica, but we were never close as siblings should be. She wasn't raised in my household and our mothers did not get along. Therefore, I didn't get to see her very often. I do have memories of the few times that we did get to spend together. Erica was a brilliant scholar and a very beautiful woman. She was a highly educated, well known, and a loved member of the community. She passed away young at the age of 37 from breast cancer. Before that, she earned several college degrees at some highly respected and prestigious universities. I wish we could have been closer, but the love I have for her remains the same. To this day, I still claim her as my own. No matter what, she was still my sister!

Tera, on the other hand, was like a second mother and father to me. She watched over my brothers and me almost every day while my Mom was at work to support four children. My sister took great care of us and taught me many significant life lessons. I could talk to her about things that I couldn't discuss with my Mother, for instance, girls and puberty. Tera was very nurturing, but she was tough when she needed to be as well. I believe the love that Tera showered me with was the affection she too had desired from my Mother but wasn't getting. I always had a healthy fear and respect for Tera's heavy-handed punches. She could frog punch you with her knuckles and cause "hickies" that would immediately spring up above the skin from the point of impact. A hickey is a bump that raises above the skin surface after being struck forcefully. She also tickled me into submission several times, and it helped me build immunity to tickling. The story behind my name is that my Dad spoiled the mess out of my sister Tera. When I was born, my sister loved the names Polo and Pierre, so my father allowed my middle name to be Pierre. Shortly after that, he bought her a dog and named it Polo. I still find humour in this story and the fact that my middle name could have easily been Polo. I prefer Pierre because it is unique and gave me my own identity, especially with the amount of Eric's within the family;

this prevented me from turning my head every time someone called out the name "Eric."

My sister Tera played a big role in my childhood and adolescence. Before she became old enough to follow in the family legacy of doing hair, I would accompany her to many social events she was involved in. This included cheerleading practice, softball practice, and Young Life. My sister was quite the athlete and I would enjoy watching her perform. She was an excellent caregiver and a social butterfly amongst her peers. She would love on me abundantly, and that contributed to me having high self-esteem and confidence. Tera was also a great cook who often prepare creative meals, which she entitled "Masterpieces." No matter what she mixed the meals would always result in a tasty and appetizing dinner. Tera enforced the house seniority rules and made sure that we did our chores daily. Tera was always there for me and in my corner while I was growing up. In my opinion, Tera raised me and always has been my biggest supporter in the world.

Tera was also responsible for introducing me to hip hop and rap music. During my childhood, my Mother would censor the music played at the house. I was not allowed to possess any music that was considered explicit. Once my sister started driving she would play songs and records that I had never heard before. The tunes were catchy and talked about many of the things that I was witnessing around me. The hard baselines and rhythms spoke directly to my soul. I quickly was drawn towards the rap artist Tupac and Jay-Z. I was influenced by their music, the intelligence in their lyrics, and their opposition to the oppression and authority. I still remember those car rides to middle school with my sister. Tera exposing me to rap opened my eyes to a world that I never knew existed.

Rico and Ricardo are fraternal twins who were born five minutes apart. Rico is five minutes older than Ricardo. My Mother initially wanted to name my brother Ricardo, "Chico."

My brother Rico was born with a rare disease called Prune Belly Syndrome. This resulted in him not developing any stomach or abdominal muscles in the womb, thus needing to wear a corset daily to support his organs. He was also born with one leg and no feet. That meant he would need a prosthesis to walk for the rest of his life. Rico spent the first four years of his life living in the hospital, which meant I spent a lot of time with Ricardo growing up. We did things most brothers do, like play video games, wrestle, argue, and fight. I have always admired Rico's toughness in dealing with his disabilities. It takes courage to have so many operations and procedures in a hospital. We would go every weekend to visit Rico in the hospital. I remember they had an arcade room, which was elaborately decked out with several games. I remember Rico's friends from the hospital would join us and play as well. Despite his challenges, Rico was involved in many of the same activities that children participated in as kids. My Mom ensured that Rico had an opportunity to go to summer camps, play sports, skate, and do whatever activities we were all involved in as well.

Ricardo is the youngest child and the baby of the family. When he was young, Ricardo would cry often and throw temper tantrums. When he was enraged, he became known and the "Beaner." My uncle Topper and my Dad had nicknamed him that after witnessing his temper themselves. Ricardo and I would fight and argue as many brothers do, but we spent a lot of time together during childhood. We enjoyed the same interest and he was involved in every activity I was. In fact, Ricardo was an excellent athlete himself. He was a great pitcher in baseball and the best cornerback on his football team. I went to all of his games and witnessed him play integral roles for his teams. During childhood, he was a tremendous trumpet player as well. He could produce clear and sharp notes even at a young age.

My twin brothers would often team up on me in situations when someone was about to get in trouble. With those odds, it was nearly impossible for me to defend myself in an argument. They both would declare, "Pierre is messing with me," and I would therefore get in trouble. My brothers would never really explain or describe what I was doing. My Mother was on her job, so she became frustrated whenever she was disturbed by our brotherly quarrels. As the eldest brother, I was always held responsible for my brothers and myself. Early in life, I think my brothers and I were competing for attention. I did shameful things like choke my brother with my karate belt and even tried to convince Ricardo to drink pee by saying it was Mountain Dew. I'm not proud of it and I admit to being a terrible big brother during my early childhood.

One time, it was snowing outside and Ricardo and I were walking to the bus stop. My Mother had told me to hold Ricardo's hand as we walked up the hill. This was his first year in school, so I must have been eight years old. I ignored my Mom's instruction and began to walk to the bus stop as normal. Ricardo was behind me with his hands in his jacket because it was cold. I kept on going up the hill and he was trailing behind me about ten feet away. I looked back and saw was beginning to lose his balance on the icy cement. All of sudden, he slipped and fell and bust his chin on the pavement. His hands were in his pockets, so he had no chance of breaking his fall. I ran back to him and he was crying and bleeding. I felt horrible! I picked him up and carried him home screaming for my Mother's help. She came outside dramatically demanding to know what happened. I told her that "*he fell*" and yelled at me for disobeying her orders. She took possession of Ricardo and the ambulance was called. Ricardo received stitches for his chin and it is a story I can never forget. It affected me deeply and was the beginning of me learning responsibility. After that, my disobedience was corrected and I made an effort to be better and protect my brothers from danger. I started to take my job as a big brother much more serious.

My Mother has always been a beautiful and hard-working woman. As a kid, I grew up knowing that she had a younger brother nick-named Topper and an older sister Debbie. My Mom did not have tons of education, but that did not prevent her from becoming a savvy and successful businesswoman. Regardless of her income, we children always were dressed in clean and fashionable clothes. My Mom had an excellent sense of style, which she inherited from her parents. We learned as kids that the name brands on clothes were not important, and that style depended on how well you could put together matching clothing items. She would always emphasize the importance of education and insisted we did well in school. My Mother would tell me how smart I was much before I realized it myself. I remember her coming home several nights after work and preparing dinner for us. I thank God for the many sacrifices my Mom made for her children.

Mom would also spank us when she was really upset. I stayed in mischief in my youth, so I likely deserved the discipline I received. I earned my fair share of spankings from my Mother. At the time, my Mom's whippings were frightening because of the theatrics and dramatics she included. She would yell, name call, curse, and sound like a broken record with each lash of the belt. I figured out as I got older that she would stop once we started crying. My Mom was forced to be the disciplinarian, even as a small petite woman. She spanked us for as long as she could to keep us in line. I grew big enough over the years to grab the belt when she swung it towards me. Soon after that, I felt like I was too big to be getting whooped by a little small lady. I once threatened to run away when I was a teenager, but my Mom was not going for it. She grabbed a bat, stood beside the door in a batting stance, and then dared me to try to leave. Wisely, I chose to remain in the house that particular night.

My Dad loved his children dearly. He came from a large family and was the 10th child out of 11 children. He was a 5'11 foot tall, light-skinned, well-groomed, handsome, charismatic, as well as a charming man. He had an infectious smile and shared laughter that would always energize and bring joy to others. The name 'Isaacs' translates into the word "laughter," and my Dad represented this correlation in the way he lived his life. He was down to earth, relatable, and was considered to be everybody's favorite uncle and family member. My Dad was extremely smart, talented, detailed, and fiercely dangerous at times. He was respected by people in the community despite his struggles with drugs. He was a highly functional addict, and you could not tell by looking at him that he was battling his own personal demons. Although he was not always physically present, my love and affection for him were unchanged. He made sure that we children knew that he loved us, and that sentiment was surely received. Eric James Isaacs had a special knack for loving his family, bringing joy to others, fighting, and attracting beautiful women.

Growing up, I spent a lot of time with my cousins on my Mom's side of the family. My Aunt Rea was the sister of my Grandma Sarah. We would sometimes go over to her house to visit or for us boys to get our haircut by Aunt Rea's son Ernie. When Ernie wasn't around, her son Marcus would cut our hair for us. I remember playing video games with her son Aaron and her daughter Julia was always sleepy.

I did spend countless hours with my cousins Twanda, Tanisha, and Theressa; Twanda was the oldest, Tanisha was slightly older than me, and Theressa was my brothers' ages. My Aunt Pat on my Mom's side of the family would watch me when my Mother was at work. They had roaches in their apartment, but my Aunt Pat took good care of me when I was with her. Tanisha was my favorite cousin during my childhood. We got along great and were around the same age of development. We went to teen clubs and would dance with each other when there was no one to dance with. My Aunt Pat had a son in early forties named DeShonte. When he was old, he joined us boys in wrestling and became known as Picante the Warrior.

Another cousin I spent a lot of time with was my cousin Eric. We had the same name and very similar interest growing up. We enjoyed hanging out together and always requested to go over his house. We played video games and played with action figures all day long. Eric had a sister name Essence and he did not like her trying to impede in our playtime. I didn't mind having her around and would teach her how to play the games we played. Eric also had a pet turtle named Lion King. I was always fascinated with his turtle because my Mother was against having animals in the house.

My cousin Deondre was an extended family member, but a family member indeed. He grew up on the same street as my Mom's salon, so we spent time together during my childhood and teenage years. Deondre liked to push the limits and always got into trouble. We played sports together and would fight each other for fun. We really were just testing each other's strength and letting off some testosterone. I was mostly with Deondre when I was active in the streets. He is the cousin that I knew would fight for me if I needed him to.

My Aunt Debbie would watch us often on the weekends or during breaks in school. She always lived in rougher neighborhoods and had drug problems that she was dealing with recovering from. Her oldest kids were Nay Nay and Tamaine. They were not living with my Aunt Debbie during my childhood, but I was close to both of them. Nay Nay would sometimes babysit me at my Grandma's apartment. She had a jerry curl and made the best home fries I ever tasted. Tamaine was smart, athletic, and had a reputation in the streets. No matter what he was involved in, Tamaine was always family oriented and I respected him. I still remember him giving me fifty dollars one Christmas. My Aunt Debbie's apartments were always crowded by roaches. They would fall from the ceiling and run out of any food that was left around. You had to check any food you ate for roaches first. Growing up, I thought that having roaches was a normal part of life. My brothers and I spent the most time with CJ, Woe Woe, and Shaq because of our closeness in our ages.

I did have two stepbrothers named Decky and Stevie. Decky was my age and Stevie was about the same brother's age as Rico and Ricardo. Decky was friendly and we got along well. We accepted each other and he eventually started playing for my football team. He wasn't very skilled, but that did not stop him from trying. Stevie was quiet when he was young and had the deepest voice of any kid I knew. We weren't connected by blood, but we have always claimed each other as brothers. They wrestled with us whenever they came over to visit.

I grew to love several people who were weren't family, but they could have been no closer. One of those people was my babysitter Ms. Mary. I remember every day when I showed up, Ms. Mary would ask me if I wanted hot or cold cereal. I always choose hot cereal, which was her specialty Crème of Wheat. It was delicious each day and when I grew older I asked her how she made it so good. She taught me the recipe. She also taught me how to skin fish. One time, my church had taken all of the young men fishing. We all returned with several fish, so I took them to Ms. Mary's house. She taught me step by step how to gut and clean a fish. I still remember those instructions today. Ms. Mary could be nice, but she would discipline kids with spankings vigorously. Her whippings hurt and she used a wooden meter stick to spank kids on the rear end. I still loved Ms. Mary and she jokingly reminded me of those spankings even as I got older.

Another person who was considered family was Ms. Phyllis. She too was my Grandma Sarah's close friend and she was present during my childhood. She had a daughter named Kim, and Kim had a son name Mike. He was a bigger guy, but younger than I and we grew up as cousins. We played together at Phyllis's house and sometimes at the beauty salon. I took him under my wing as my cousin and we had great times playing during childhood. My brothers and I gave him the affectionate nickname of "Mikey Mildew." I don't really remember him being smelly, but I do know that he wasn't fazed by the name and embraced it.

Ms. Mays was a lady from my church, but she also got her hair done by my mother. In fact, her daughter did as well and they both frequented the shop routinely. Ms. Mays was not only a lead choir member, but she was also in charge of the church's summer camp for kids. For many years, my family and I lived right next to Golden Leaf Baptist church. Due to proximity and divine nature, my brothers and I became active members in the church. During that time, Ms. Mays provided me with an oversight and love that is hard not mention.

The last member of my family that I want to mention is my church. I spent years being involved in the church choir, band, summer camp, and activities. I played the trombone for the church, but I never really received any formal training for the instrument. I went home and practiced on my own until I could produce some predictable high and low tones. I made several friendships with the other kids in the church and many of those have lasted over the years. All of the people I grew up with in the church still refer to each other as brother and sister. The women of the church looked actively advised the kids and deacons tried to teach how to be kingdom men. The pastor Reverend Atkins knew my Grandma Sarah and had a deep and captivating voice.

As a kid, if I could not receive the word from the sermons, then I could definitely receive it from the singing. The choir was outstanding under Sister Berry's direction. She once made me sing a solo and I didn't do awful, but I wouldn't say I did great. My Mom came that Sunday and didn't seem too impressed. No matter what, I enjoyed singing for the Lord and relationships I developed within the church. I remember being able to tell when church was about to be over because he would end every sermon saying, "**All Power, In His Hand!**" He would repeat it several times, but once he said it he was headed towards the Benediction. The amount of time I spent in the church during my childhood and adolescent years would equate to that of a family member.

I thank God for all of the family he blessed me with. I realize I am fortunate to even know who many of my family members were. I appreciate and have learned from the connections and memories we shared. I love each of my family members for different reasons, but equally. I can only accept them for whatever good or bad they may have done in my life. My family helped me realize who I was and gave me a foundation to build upon. I am grateful for how God used my family to show me His love.

Top Left: Tera Lee Isaacs, Teresa Isaacs Bottom Left: Eric
Pierre Isaacs, Rico Alonzo Isaacs, Eric James Isaacs, Ricardo
Alfonzo Isaacs

Chapter 4

Do No Harm

"Beloved, I pray that all may go well with you and that you may be in good health, as it goes well with your soul." 3 John 2

The doctors told my Mother that my brother Rico would not live to see twenty-four hours. My Mother prayed to Jesus and asked for his healing touch in sparing my brother's life. Thankfully, my brother became a living miracle for me to witness with my own eyes. I am happy to report that Rico has lived well into his thirties. From an early age, I learned that God could do things that other people deemed impossible.

Rico spent the first years of his life in the hospital, but when he turned four years old he came home to live with us permanently. When he came home, he wasn't alone. He had nurses in our house around the clock caring for him. It was an adjustment for the entire family, but we grew comfortable with the nurses being in the house day and night. These lovely ladies practically lived with us and made huge impressions on me and the entire family in numerous ways. Accordingly, the Lord used these nurses to stretch and challenge my schemas as a young man.

The first nurse that ever showed up at our house was named Lori Leutsch. She was a healthy, full-figured woman and she was as sweet as pie. She loved her country music, her pugs, her tomato sandwiches, and most memorably she loved our family like we were her own. Early on in life, I learned that love would come in all shapes, sizes, and colors. When she would be working on shift, Lori would often take Rico to different places and allowed my brother Ricardo and me to attend as well. Lori was the nicest lady, but she had behavioral expectations and rules for us in public. When we were in Lori's car, she did not allow us to change her radio station to the rap station we were familiar with. She insisted we learned to adjust and listen to the country music she liked since it was her vehicle. We were hesitant and defensive at first, but over time I began to appreciate the storytelling in country music.

Lori took us, boys, to all sorts of outings like the movies, the mall, and restaurants. LaRosa's pizza was one of her favorite dining facilities to eat at. Lori lived in the country and had two dogs named Julio and Ornery. Her husband was a grumpy old man by the name of George. I remember her taking us to her house way outside of town. It didn't take long for me to embrace the calm and serenity offered by the countryside. It was peaceful and quiet, which was a huge difference from what I had experienced in the city. Lori was the first nurse to work at our house and also the last nurse to work a shift for Rico, years later when he no longer required nurses. I'm thankful for her because she provided me with an alternative perspective, lifestyle, and culture. Lori was phenomenal at her job and treated my family with love and compassion.

Another nurse Rico had that made a huge impact on my life was Jane Day. Although she was a wealthy woman, she had a very down to earth and practical spirit about herself. In my opinion, Jane Day was a guardian angel sent directly from above. I remember she taught us kids the Lords' prayer, and we practiced it daily until we had it memorized. From that time forward, we said a prayer every night before going to bed. She was the type of person that would always tell me the truth. I remember one time she gave me some sound advice regarding one of my friends in the neighborhood. Jane informed me about how he wasn't being a good friend and that he was treating me unfairly. She cautioned me about my undying loyalty and affinity towards him. Jane advised me to recognize how he was "acting funny" towards me. I wasn't ready to accept it initially, but shortly after I learned she was absolutely right.

Jane also made a huge impact because of a gift that she gave me. One time, my brothers and I were at Jane's house and she was having a garage sale and party. She invited my entire family out to her house to go swimming and have dinner. As the early evening approached, the garage sale was winding down and coming to an end. I noticed two pairs of skates laying near the front of the garage. The two remaining pairs of skates belonged to her daughters, who no longer needed the high-quality blades. They were gold on the outside with purple wheels, so they definitely caught my attention. I asked if I could try them on and Jane responded by saying, "You can have them." I was shocked and kindly replied, "*Thank you!*"

Ironically, both pairs of skates were perfect fits for my brother Ricardo and me. They were professionally styled rollerblades and were extremely fast. I remember Ricardo and me zipping down the driveway while trying them out. Skating instantly became a favorite and preferred pastime of mine. I would skate down hills, streets, steps, and any other terrain. These amazing golden skates played a significant role in my development. For that reason alone, Jane's memory is forever etched in my heart. She gave me a gift that kept on giving. Skating provided me with an expressive and constructive outlet for my youthful energy.

Josette was another nurse who stayed long enough to make an impact on my family. She was younger than Lori and Jane and had a large family of her own. She was a curvaceous reddish-brunette with plenty of spunk about herself and an attractive personality. She would invite my brothers and me to her house weekly for movie and pizza nights. We had these just about every weekend Josette was working on shift. I remember her having a blended family with her new husband, Tim. They had several children combined, which always led to a lot of fun and engaging kid-friendly activities. The fun attached to those experiences during childhood is the reason I even remember them. The movie nights we had were epic adventures and all the kids together had a blast!

Tim was a Native American and Caucasian fellow. He was an amazing left-handed artist, who could draw elaborate and detailed photographs with precision. I remember him drawing much of the time we were over Josette's house visiting. I gave him some respect based on his expertise with paper and pencil. Tim was small in stature, so he had a short man's complex, a temper issue, and an anger problem. I could tell he didn't like the idea of my brothers and I being at the house all the time.

My brothers would sometimes tease Tim, which would cause him to lose his temper. It was hilarious for me to watch my twin brothers have so much control and influence over an adult. Rico, Ricardo, and I would randomly say lines from movies and then joke and laugh about it. Tim always would assume that my brothers were making fun of him in some kind of way. Even though we were just reciting the lines from movies, he didn't like it! One time it made Tim feel a certain way. On this day, my brothers were saying phrases like, "You raaaaaaang" and "Hey Stoup!" Those were famous lines from the movies Little Giants and Coming to America, but it made Tim furious. Tim clearly did not understand the random lines being recited or what was causing us to laugh so hysterically.

Tim became angry and told my brother, Rico, "You keep talking boy and I'm going to stick my four fingers through your shoulder blades." We burst into laughter! Due to his accent and small size, my brothers and I were not intimidated by his threats. In fact, his response took on a life of its own. My brother Rico decided to "remix" the words shoulder blades. Once we eventually stop laughing, my brother Rico retorted, *"shou-shou-shou-shoulder blades shoulder blades."* We again burst into laughter, as Tim was outraged by his words being used against him. My brother Ricardo joined in the fun by mocking, *"shou-shou-shou-shoulder blades."* We thought it pure comedy and hilarious. We all would laugh out loud uncontrollably whenever someone would say it. Tim complained to Josette about us making fun of him, and we were asked to leave Tim alone. We did as we were told, but it instantly became a classic catchphrase.

Tim contributed to another brotherly catchphrase when he was once again aggravated and heated about something Rico was laughing about. If someone was laughing, Tim would automatically assume the laughter was about him. I'm not sure what Rico was laughing at, but Tim responded to Rico by saying, "I can accomplish more than you can accomplish!" This threat also became a common comical phrase that we repeated. Whenever we had the opportunity, one of us brothers would say, *"I can accomplish more than you can accomplish!"* We would all laugh out loud hysterically. Tim, with the intuition from his complex, knew that he was being made fun of. He would try hard not to be involved in the weekend activities, but Josette would convince him sometimes to participate.

During one visit, Josette's youngest son Brandon and my youngest brother Ricardo were playing together, but it escalated into a scrap. They were around the same age and size, so I saw no need to intervene at the time. Brandon and Ricardo were arguing about something, and the two got into a small scuffle. My brothers and I wrestled all the time together, including my disabled brother Rico. When Ricardo and Brandon got into a tussle, my brother Ricardo got the upper hand easily. Ricardo scooped him off his feet and threw Brandon to the ground. Brandon got up and continued to thrust forward toward Ricardo. Ricardo threw one punch, which landed squarely on Brandon's nose. The results were tears and a bloody nose for Brandon. I recollect Brandon flailing in defense and Josette not being able to stomach the situation. It seemed like a good match from my view. After that incident, we were no longer allowed to go over to Josette's house. Nevertheless, Josette was still special for the care she provided for my family and the memorable times at her house.

There were a few other nurses that weren't able to maintain their employment at my house for various reasons. One of the most notorious nurses was named Shirley. She was an elderly white lady and had an odd kind of personality. She looked mean and cranky all the time, but she was nice for the most part. Shirley loved to eat pea soup! She offered some to me one time, and I hesitated to try it. I pretended to gag from considering the idea, but I eventually did give it a chance. It tasted like any vegetable soup would to a kid, *disgusting*. Shirley would, of her own desire, walk throughout the house gathering everyone's laundry to wash. That began to rub my Mother in the wrong way. Shirley would even go into my Mom and Stepdad's room to retrieve personal articles of clothing. My Mother didn't like the idea of Shirley going into her room and grabbing Creester's underwear. I remember hearing my Mom gossip about the offense later.

Shirley was supposed to my brother's nurse, but it was in her nature to take care of everyone around her. One time, Shirley ask my Stepdad, "Do you want a sandwich, Creester?" He laughed out loud and welcomed the idea kindly by replying, "Yes Shirley, thank you! I would like a sandwich. Hahaha!" He chuckled about the pampering and my Mother took offense to Shirley tampering in her relationship. After that, my Mom finally complained to Lori about Shirley's behavior. Lori handled the issue and Shirley was removed from Rico's case shortly thereafter. I remember Shirley having a bad headache on her last shift working at the house. Creester had to escort her to her car because she was having such a hard time. I gazed through the window blinds, concerned about her safely getting home. That was the last I saw of Shirley.

Another nurse that didn't pan out well was Deb. She was a heavy-set woman with glasses and I recall her being extremely paranoid. I remember she would take Rico's Ensure protein drinks from the supply at my house and give them to her daughter as supplements for meals. She was concerned that her young daughter was gaining too much weight too quickly. Deb asked my Mom for a case, and she gave it to her. My Mother grew concerned because she thought Deb wasn't feeding her daughter any real food. Deb was an extremely anxious and paranoid person, so my Mother found her behavior odd from the start.

Deb would also openly express that she thought she was seeing ghosts at our townhouse. Us boys, not understanding reflections, would be frightened by the darts of light in our window. One of us boys commented that we saw a ghost, and Deb alertly said, "What!" Her eyes got big and she was on edge from that point forward. Now, I realize the "ghost" we believed to see was merely a reflection from the car lights pulling into our parking lot. However, anytime there was a reflection, Deb would apprehensively uphold that she saw a ghost. You better believe, "*I think I saw a ghost*," became another comical catchphrase between my brothers and me. Deb confessed her suspicions to my Mother, and soon after she was no longer working on Rico's case either.

One time, there was a temporary nurse who took my brother and me out to her house for dinner. She lived in a racist neighborhood, and I was instantly harassed when I went outside to play. This was my first experience with someone openly not liking me because of my skin color. Once we arrived at her house, her son, Tyler, asked me if I wanted to ride bikes and I happily agreed. The family had several bikes in the garage, so I picked one out that liked and hopped onto it. While riding, Tyler asked me if I would be interested in riding to pick up a few of his other friends. I was having a good time, so I agreed and we rode further down the street away from his house. Tyler was excited about taking me to meet and play with his friends.

The next thing I know, we get near Tyler's friend's house and there are three other boys riding bikes. We approach them and the looks on their faces were unforgettable. They were upset at Tyler for bringing me around to ride bikes with them. The posse of boys began circling around me on their bikes, screaming, "Nigger, nigger, nigger!" I had heard the word used before, but this time was different. There was a condemnation attached to it and it instantly offended me. I was infuriated by the remark and got off of my bike to chase after them and fight. They keep their distance and just laughed and mocked me continuously from their bikes. Tyler asked them to stop, but they scolded him for riding bikes with me and bringing me around. They told Tyler that he was no longer their friend and they didn't want to play with him anymore. He was distraught and began riding his bike home. I got back on the bike and followed him. He was upset and crying on that ride home, with me trailing a short distance behind.

Once we arrived back at the house, the nurse was concerned to see her son sobbing as he came through the door. She asked what was wrong and he told her that his friends said they weren't playing with him anymore because of me. The nurse not only lived in a racist neighborhood, but she was in fact racist herself. She actually blamed me for the incident and never allowed me to come back to her house. I showed up and was called a "Nigger," so I didn't understand how it was my fault. I felt like my anger in the situation was justified. However, the kid in me felt sorry to be involved with Tyler losing his friends. The nurse was just temporary, so she didn't work for us long. She is so insignificant to me that I don't even remember her name. But I will never forget the incident.

There were many more nurses along the way, but the ones I discussed were the most memorable. An overwhelming amount of them affected my childhood in a positive way. Although these ladies were my brother's nurses, they loved on all of my family. I was thankful for the experiences I had with them, the nurturing, and their protection during my childhood years. The nurses were not only responsible for my brother Rico, but they contributed so much more. These amazing women were blessings to my upbringing and heaven-sent. A nurse taught me how to pray, how to recognize a bad friend, how to use manners in public, and how to explore other worlds. Those ladies showed me that love comes in all sizes, shapes, and colors. I did learn that there was a difference between white and black, but I also learned that both colors love the same way.

Chapter 5

Roller Blades and Golden Skates

"You make known to me the path of life; in your presence, there is fullness of joy; at your right hand are pleasures forever-more." **Psalm 16:11**

The skates my brother and I received from Rico's nurse Jane played a major part in our childhoods. We skated around the neighborhood, around the city, and even to my Mother's job miles away. These golden skates were very high quality and lasted us for years. The skates were the fastest in-line rollerblades that I have ever seen in my life. My brother and I simply removed the cushions from inside of them when our feet outgrew the skates to give us another couple of years of riding them. We would wear thick layers of socks instead of the manufacturer's cushions to preserve space. They were the greatest pair of skates a boy could ever wish for.

We would ride our blades down staircases and every hill we would come across. We even played basketball in our skates and street hockey whenever we could corral enough kids to have a game. At one point, my Mother's salon was down the street from a local roller rink called the Fun Factory. My brother and I would ask permission to go skating each weekend when we had to go with my Mom to work. She would always agree to let us go and we went to the roller rink unsupervised. We enjoyed being able to skate, dance, and play games at the roller rink, so we always behaved. The time spent skating allowed me to hone in on my skating skills as well as develop physically. My legs were muscular, which allowed me to be fast and have stamina while running and playing sports. My brother and I had so much fun on our skates that our joy impacted other kids in the neighborhood. Before we knew it, more and more kids had begun skating in the neighborhood.

Golden Skates was actually the name of a skating rink that played a major part in my adolescence. Golden Skates, for most teens in Cincinnati, Ohio, was like a rite of passage. I remember watching my sister and her friends go to the teen dances to have a good time each holiday weekend. My Mother worked, so my sister had to take me with her to many of the social events that she went to. One of those places was Golden Skates. There were portions of the night where skating occurred when my sister's generation went, but by the time my generation went, there was no more skating, just bumping and grinding.

The holiday teen dances they host were extremely popular, which was evident by the number of kids that would show up. It seemed as if every cool kid and teen in the city would attend the holiday dances. Before the doors opening, a long line would form outside in anticipation. Rain, sleet, or snow, every teen in the city was determined to get inside. For people who went often, you could look at the line and tell if the event was likely to reach capacity. Before you enter, the Police would want you to ensure you were not carrying any drugs or weapons, so everyone was patted down. Extra security was necessary because every event night there were approximately 10 to 15 fights.

Each holiday there was a themed dance, with the major holidays having the best events. Yes, there was a lot of grinding going on, but at least it was something safe to do in the city. It did not matter how much Golden Skates charged for entrance. The kids would still pay the fee without caution. When my sister was going it cost $5 to get in. Soon after it went up to $8 per kid. I inherited skating when it was at $10, but soon became $12 and then $15 to get in. The kids still paid! You would think that this was too much money to pay, however, the dances often reached capacity and would have to stop letting people in. It was important to get there early, so you were not left out due to capacity.

Once you enter, people would put their coats in the quarter lockers if they had them. The boys would immediately begin to circle the dance floor. Kids wore their cleanest outfits and represented their neighborhoods throughout the evening. The girls would link up with their groups in the middle of the dance floor and begin to taunt the boys for attention. Everyone was waiting for the DJ to transition from basic music to the hardcore club hits that energized many of the kids to fight and freak dance. When a hype song came on, people would represent their neighborhoods, gangs, and communities by corralling and throwing up signs in the promotion of their cliques. Besides that, what we were doing long ago at Golden Skates commonly became known as "twerking." I grew with an appreciation for Rap and R&B music early on because of my sister, but Golden Skates exposed me to much more music. The type of music that would not have been welcomed in my household. I learned that some music goes with pain, some songs were made for love, and others were made to get the party started.

I was always nervous or anxious that I might be caught up in a fight at Golden Skates. However, I never had to fight and got to enjoy Golden Skates every time. I played several sports, so I knew quite a few people from around the city and multiple neighborhoods. My secret formula was paying more attention to the girls. I would make eye contact with the guys to let them know I wasn't scared, but whenever my eye needed to wander I would focus on finding the nearest prettiest girl. Not making eye contact with someone was a sign of weakness. I circled the rink looking for old friends that I had known and I would give them a pound or handshake and say, "*What's up?*" I would also flash smiles at girls that I anticipated dancing with at some point during the evening.

Golden Skates was a kid version of the club. The DJ would control the energy of the evening and whenever there were too many fights, he would put on slow songs to try to calm down the hormonal energy. Most of the time people would not fight because they had a problem with someone. Mainly, fights happened because someone wanted to draw attention to themselves or impress a certain group of girls. Different neighborhoods would have issues with each other for some reason or another. Either way, wisdom taught me to travel with a group whenever I attended. Even if the people that were with you could not fight, there was strength in numbers. Having a group with you meant that you were less likely to be bothered.

Everyone would just wait in anticipation for the DJ to play the first high-energy song. One of those songs bound to get the party started was "No Limit Soldiers" by Master P. Another song was "Drag'Um to the River" by UNLV. Another song the DJ would commonly play was "Freak Hoes" by Master P as well. Any three of those songs were guaranteed to excite the crowd and ignite the energy inside the rink. During this time, No Limit was the dominant rap label of the time. Down south music was just coming on to the scene. Cincinnati, however, was on cue with the initial wave and popularity of the budding genre. Southern music played a big part in my adolescence; it was emerging at the same time as my puberty.

When the first rowdy song was played, the boys would dash towards the girls they had been scoping that night to dance with. The girls would start twerking (shaking their butts) and that was an indicator that they were willing to dance with someone. Although, you had to prove yourself worthy bypassing a few tests. The girls gave each boy a test that included three main objectives. First, you had to pass the shoe test. While a girl was dancing, you would approach the girl from the rear and the first thing she would do is look down at your shoes. If your shoes were acceptable she would continue to dance. Next, if you passed the first test, she would dance for a few moments and check out your rhythm. It was important to hold your ground and not get bounced backward by a girl. It was taken as a sign of weakness if a girl could back you up from your original position. Girls and guys commonly referred to this action as getting "twerked up" or "bucking." If the young lady liked how you moved, the third test was the look on your face. This was the most difficult step in the process. If you were ugly or too excited, the girl might ridicule you with a facial expression or laugh. Sometimes, they would be nice about it and continue to dance, but discreetly move away from you. Many times the girls were not so nice and would frown, name call you, then move away from you in frustration. I saw many guys get bucked off because they were too eager or excited. Haha!

It was every boys' goal those nights to get on something and stay on it. If you found five or more girls that would dance with you, that was considered a good night. I was handsome, athletic, and fashionable, so I always did well at Golden Skates. Most of us young men were aroused during the dances. Some girls did not mind it and would actually take it as an insult if guys were not aroused while dancing with them. The girls would commonly refer to this as the boy being "on bone". I quickly learned very deceptive ways to hide and mask my puberty infused erections. I learned to tuck my penis underneath my belt in my pants, so if a girl said that I was "hard," I would counter, "that is a belt buckle." Luckily for me, I never really ran into that issue, but that was my automatic defense.

I always had a blast at the holiday dances. I can only remember being rejected a few times out of all the years that I went. There, I learned to deal with my insecurities and doubts. It made me deal with the real possibility of rejection and it also taught me how to bounce back immediately. The worst a girl can say is "no." If a girl was unwilling to dance with me, more than likely, her friend right next to her might say, "Yes." Boys learned the importance of grooming themselves and displaying confidence in their appearance. I'm sure some of the girls learned how to lure boys, be respected, and how to keep a guys' attention. We were all in the same phase of life and learning from our social environment.

Overall, Golden Skates was a great opportunity for the youth in the city of Cincinnati. The teen dances provided us with somewhere to express our hearts' desires and release energy that we would otherwise not know what to do with. Aside from the imminent threat of fighting, these events gave the kids in the city an outlet and a relatively safer alternative to running the streets. I learned a lot about people and most certainly tons about myself. I prayed to God to guard me against all those crazy fights and he certainly did. I asked God to shield me from any harm being done and I always left unscathed. I thank God for his protection, the experiences, and how instrumental it was in my formation as an adolescent.

Roller Blades and Roller Skates

Chapter 6

The Incredible Oz

"Yea, though I walk through the valley of the shadow of death, I will fear no evil: for thou art with me; thy rod and thy staff they comfort me." **Psalms 23:4**

After my paternal grandfather exposed me to wrestling, it started my love for sports entertainment, and I became a die-hard fan of the then-known-as World Wrestling Federation (now WWE), World Championship Wrestling (WCW), and Extreme Championship Wrestling (ECW). My infatuation with wrestling lasted throughout my childhood and adolescent years. I shared my wrestling experience with my brothers and my cousins, who became huge pro wrestling fans as well. Any boy family member that was in our vicinity had no choice but to be influenced by our love for wrestling adventures.

My older sister Tera loved wrestling entertainment too. She would watch it on television and knew several of the characters. My paternal Grandfather may have sparked the interest, but it was definitely my sister who keep the legacy going. When I was young, Tera would randomly attack me by pinning me down and forcing me to fight out. She would say, *"Shut up punk"*, in a joking manner and drop an elbow on me if I whined or screamed to get out. Her secret weapon and finishing move was a Tickle Attack. While pinned down to the ground or bed, Tera would tickle me into submission and I eventually became immune by building up a tolerance. I still was no match for Tera.

Many of the wrestling stars were role models for me growing up and I found a connection to their fictional personas. My favorite characters were the All-American Hulk Hogan, the Macho Man Randy Savage, the Ultimate Warrior, and Superfly Jimmy Snuka. I was thrilled when Hacksaw Jim Duggan would come down the aisle with a two by four yelling, "Hoooooo!" I felt a bolt of energy whenever the Big Boss Man would twirl his nightstick. I trembled when Earthquake would do his stomp and danced when Koko B. Ware would come to the ring with his bird. Whenever my Aunt Pat babysat us, we would watch the special events on pay per view. We would sit around the television while eating dinner and enjoy the entertainment. I still remember all of the wrestlers and recognize their lasting impact on my childhood.

Not only did we watch the shows, but we would also practice many of the moves and imitated everything we saw. When all together, we would instantly throw down some couch cushions and start wrestling. We managed to avoid major injury most of the time, even though we were pulling off very complicated moves. We knew how to execute moves like body slams and power-bombs, with as little damage as possible. When one of us caught chicken pocks, we all caught it at the same time because we could not resist the temptation to wrestle. We scrapped all day long until we broke something or until one of the adults would yell at us to stop. An adult would yell, "*Sit yawl asses down somewhere; it sounds like the roof is caving in!*" Being tired was rarely a reason that we ever stopped, as our adventures lasted well into the evening hours.

My brothers and I were very close to my Aunt Debbie's younger boys and we spent a lot of time with them growing up. It was a royal rumble anytime my cousins CJ, Woe Woe, and Shaq were around. All three of them were phenomenal athletes in all the sports they participated in. My cousin CJ was the oldest of Aunt Debbie's younger boys. He was small in stature but tough and quick, so he took on the persona of a high flying wrestler. My cousin Woe Woe was slightly younger than CJ but very similar in skills, abilities, and persona. Shaq was the youngest boy, yet he was the stockiest and strongest of the three boys. Shaq would eat more than his brothers, so he outgrew them at a young age and he took on the persona of a power wrestler. My brother Ricardo's wrestling persona was Vicky Vale, who was a hot-headed ladies' man. He had tons of personality, charisma, and was a talented wrestler as well. Even my handicapped brother Rico joined in on the fun and became known as the wrestling sensation Meeble. We all made certain to protect Rico's disabilities but we included him in our physical roughhousing. We all were hooked!

My cousins, brothers, and I had entrance music, personas, costumes, and finishing moves. My wrestling nickname was The Incredible Oz. I was raised in the church, so my finishing move was fittingly called the Benediction. I took on the personality of a championship wrestler and used my age and size to dominate my younger cousins and brothers. I made sure to let them get in moves as well and carry out whatever storyline they chose to follow for themselves. It made us tougher, and we all became very skilled wrestlers because of it. Even today, that practice and time we spent loving the sport are ingrained in the souls.

One time during a holiday, we took full advantage of everyone being centrally located at the time. We decided to have our own pay per view event and video recorded it. Our wrestling federation was called EHW or Extreme Hard-core Wrestling.

We came to the conclusion that the event would be called "EHW Beef." The wrestling episode included wreckage, entertainment, and blood. We all went to the extreme for the camera. We slammed each other through boxes like they were wooden tables. We hit each other over the head with clothes hampers pretending they were steel trash cans. We jumped off of furniture like they were the top turn-buckles. Everything was going great until my cousin Woe Woe's nose started bleeding. He started crying and we paused to make sure he was okay, but the adults were alerted and the action was cancelled for that night. I wish I still had that tape!

I always understood that real wrestlers consider television wrestling to be fake and strictly entertainment. I remember before each wrestling show, there would be a public service announcement: Please don't try this at home. It was for our safety as these wrestling moves are performed by trained professionals and not meant to be used by those unfamiliar with the sport or business, whatever you would call it. Despite the warning, for us, it is what we were exposed to, learned from, and utilized.

As a child, many things can seem scary. I have learned to fear nothing but God alone on this earth. I like to believe that even back then, God was using this experience to teach me some of the skills and abilities I would need to confidently defend myself. I remain very sound at wrestling and will always use it when necessary.

Illustrated by Olabode S. Ajiboye

Chapter 7

The Najee

*"If the axe is dull and its edge unsharpened, more strength is needed, but skill will bring success." **Ecclesiastes 10:10***

My Grandma, Mother, and sister were all licensed and formally trained beauticians. My Dad by trade was a barber, so being around styling hair was a major part of my childhood. Although doing hair was a tradition in my family, my Mother made it clear from the beginning that being a beautician was not an option as a career path for me. It didn't take much convincing either. I learned early on that styling hair was not within my gifts and abilities.

I remember a time back when I was eleven or twelve years old. I wrongfully assumed that the art of styling hair was an ability automatically passed down through genetics and that I, too, possessed the same family skills. I decided to try my hand as a barber. I borrowed a pair of my mom's clippers that I found in the bathroom cabinet. We had plenty of hair styling products and equipment laying around the house because of the family business.

I set forth on my journey to claim what was naturally mine, or so I thought. I proclaimed and bragged to the neighborhood kids that I could cut hair and was giving out free haircuts to increase my customer base. I wasn't a bad salesman at all because soon after advertising my services, a kid named Najee asked me if I could "hook him up?" I replied, "*Yes*," and he responded by saying, "Let me ask my mom!"

He lived in the townhouses directly north of my row. From my front door, his house was located about three doors to the left on the other side. He was the youngest of three brothers. His eldest brother, who was a few years younger than me, was named David. He was a brown-skinned kid with a tall and slender body frame. He was easy to get along with and was a fairly good athlete. The middle son was named Jay, and I remember him mostly by his nickname Rhino. Rhino's body type resembled and reflected his nickname as he was a stocky built kid. Najee was the youngest of the brothers, and he was a bit more heavy set for his age. He still had much of his baby fat. However, that didn't stop him from being athletic. Najee still tried to play sports and compete like every other neighborhood boy. Najee looked a lot like his mother, who had agreed to allow me to cut his hair. He would be my first ever client!

Without any practice, I met him in his basement to embark on my destiny of becoming a barber. Once settled into the make-believe barber chair, my client Najee said to me with excitement, "Give me a FILA sign!" I had no real idea about how to execute it, but I blindly responded, "*Yea, I got you.*" I had no idea what I was getting into. Nevertheless, I was good at drawing, and hairdressing was in my family. Therefore, I figured that I had a pretty good chance of being able to cut Najee's hair without a problem. Quickly, I learned that drawing and cutting hair were two very different things. I remember nervously plugging up the clippers into the outlet. With every ounce of blind confidence, I started to cut his hair and then realized early on that I may have bitten off more than I could handle. The idea and passion for succeeding were there, but the technical skills necessary to apply the desired style was not. The skill of cutting hair was much more difficult than it looked and even more than I had anticipated.

Immediately, the FILA sign idea wasn't working out as planned. I explained to him that the FILA sign was messed up, but I was still going to still "hook him up" as promised. The haircut was progressively getting worse with every stroke. It was messed up, but I tried my best to fix it and make it at least presentable. That didn't happen as planned either. Unfortunately, the repairs happened to worsen the damage, and the dream instantly became a nightmare. Najee's haircut had a mixture of knicks, scratches, and patches all over it by the time I was done cutting it. Looking back, I now realize that I was using clippers meant to trim and line up the hair for the entire haircut!

I remember the look on his mother's face when she first laid eyes on the haircut. She came downstairs smiling after cooking and playing music upstairs. However, that expression quickly changed into one of confusion and rage. Her eyes went from small to large. Her mouth was gaping open, with her eyes bulging from their sockets, and her blood pressure visibly boiling. She was in shock and speechless! I just smiled, and my naive young mind was ignorantly thinking, "I hope she likes it." With the same facial expression, his mother slowly approached Najee and used her right hand to smack his shoulder, which turned him around, allowing her to get a full view of the masterpiece. With a smile, I kindly asked: *Can I get paid?*" Now, I had her undivided attention. She was highly upset, as you can imagine, but bless her mother's heart for still paying me for the service of my failure. She could have told me that I didn't deserve it as I had ruined her son's hair, but she didn't. She then told Najee, "Grab a handful of that change from the jar upstairs on the table." Najee ran off to retrieve the bounty, which left me and her alone in the basement.

Her facial expression still had not changed from when she came down the stairs. Her eyes and mouth were wide open while she stared me down at a loss for words. Najee came tumbling down the steps and tried to give the change to his mother. She pointed to me, and Najee gave me the change. Altogether it may have totalled a dollar and twelve cents, but no matter how much it was, I had earned it! Needless to say, I figured out right then and there that hair was not something I was good at. You live and learn, so that was just another one of my life lessons.

My brothers and I still laugh about that event even today. As kids, it was so funny amongst us, and we joked and chuckled about the failed attempt every so often. Anytime we would see someone with a less than par haircut, we giggled and would say, "He has a Najee."

Through my first failed haircutting experience, God gave me guidance and direction. He knew the empathy and sympathy that I had about the profession of hairstyling. It was only natural for me to want to pursue the family legacy in some capacity or another. God allowed the Najee Experiment to make the decision clear for me. This story makes me recognize the spirit of God is always leading me towards my rightful path. My philosophy in life in regards to making a mistake or failure is that each experience presents an opportunity for change and growth. You can learn so much from your mistakes and the experience can apply later in life.

"Let the wise listen and add to their learning, and let the discerning get guidance." Proverbs 1:5

Illustrated by Eric Pierre Isaacs

Chapter 8

Beauty and Glamour

"Why, even the hairs of your head are all numbered. Fear not; you are of more value than many sparrows." **Luke 12:7**

My Grandmother was the matriarch in my family and a beautician by trade. Her love and skill for doing hair were passed down to my Mother, my sister Tera, and other members of my extended family. Grandma Sarah opened her own shop with the encouragement she received from my Grandpa. It was called the Hair Palace and was located in Bond Hill on Reading Road. Although my Grandma Sarah started the business, my Mother took over running the family salon in her prime years. At times, I do remember my family working in other businesses around town. One of those businesses was a place called Shampoo and it was located in Avondale. However, I remember my Mother owning her own salon for the majority of my childhood. My Mom's beauty salon was called Beauty and Glamour and was located in College Hill on North Bend Road. In the beginning, Creester helped Mom open the shop and set up his own photography studio in the back of the salon.

When my sister Tera grew old enough to work, I spent countless hours in *"the shop."* That was the name within my family for the beauty salon. My Grandmother, Mother, and eventually Tera all worked together in the same salon. At times, family members and people close to the family worked at the shop too. I loved seeing the familiar faces, smiling customers, and visitors that frequented the business during its prime. The shopping center's parking lot would be jammed-packed many days of the week and especially on the weekends. There was a laundry mat next door and a health food store called Twin Pines two doors down.

Many times, people would bring their kids to the beauty shop and that led to me having someone new to play with. If there was no one there for me to play with, I would use my action figures and wrestling men to explore endless adventures in my environment. Imaginative play was a big part of my childhood because it allowed me to learn, and in some ways, escape. I used my toys to climb chairs like they were mountains, jump around on plants like in the jungle, and to have epic battles on the concrete wall outside.

There were several memorable characters who I would see whenever I was at Beauty and Glamour. The first person I will mention is Norman. He was a dark-skinned stocky gentleman with a bald head. He was affectionately known as "Storming Norman" because he would walk and work at a fast and brisk pace. I now realize that Norman may have been developmentally delayed as an adult, but he seemed normal enough to me as a kid. He was always nice and would often take me to the corner store for snacks. I felt safe and protected by his presence in the shop because he was the only male who worked there. My Grandma Sarah must of had pity on Norman because she would have him clean up the shop and pay him out of her own pocket. He was a hard worker, consistent, and dependable. I enjoyed having Norman around the shop for many years in my childhood.

Another character who was familiar at the shop was LaLa. He is most memorable because of the comedic value and entertainment he provided for several years. He was a lean brown-skinned man who smiled all the time and had a shining gold tooth in the front of his mouth. I never saw LaLa not smiling. I now realize that LaLa may have been the neighborhood drunkard. He always would proclaim that he was once the lead singer for a group called The Stacktallions. He would do different melodic riffs around the shop and my brothers and I thought it was hilarious. The facial expressions he made and his conviction while singing were pure comedy to watch. He sang like he was in pain and his life depended on it. He would randomly burst into song with ad-libs like "Uh oh uuuuuuhhhhh baby!" and "IIIIIIIIiiiiiiiiiiiiiiiiiii!" My brothers and I would be rolling on the floor laughing, but that did not discourage LaLa from showcasing his talent.

LaLa had another common phrase he used when seeing us kids for the first time in the day. With a large smile, he would say "Hey little babies, give LaLa some sugar." It was weird at first, but not once we got to know him. His intentions were good of course, but I never went in for any sugar. Instead, I opted to hug him. My brothers and I would commonly mock LaLa's riffs whenever we were looking for a good laugh. If nothing else, Lala made a big enough impression on me to be remembered. Maybe he was a lead singer and superstar with the Stacktallions after all.

I used my ears and listened to the endless laughter and gossip surrounding me. I had to pretend to not be listening because it was rude for kids to be in a grown person's business. Oh, but I was listening! I learned early on to "*get out of people's mouths.*" I made lasting connections with many of the customers that frequented the business throughout the years. The women were often happy to see me and appreciated the respect that was rendered towards them. Every time I got in trouble in school or at home, it commonly became an instant topic of conversation and shop news. When something happened, the whole shop knew about it. During those times, the women would frown upon me and encourage me to do better. Needless to say, it was embarrassing and gave me the motivation to do better. I made the headlines several times!

For years, I watched as the business blossomed and the long-lasting relationships were formed. The time spent at the shop was a valuable learning lesson in business and customer service right before my eyes. The women customers would always leave feeling better than they did when they entered. The art and appreciation of women were discovered and developed during those childhood years of my life as well. I meddled in the relationship problems and conflict resolution strategies being discussed. If caught not minding my business, my Grandma Sarah would say to me, "Stop Metling!" I thought 'metling' was a real word until I learned otherwise in school. As a kid, I snooped and gathered valuable information about what women liked and what they didn't like. I listened to how certain gestures and actions from men made the women feel. An appreciation for the female perspective was developed and nurtured during this time. My time being nosey in the beauty salon gave me an advanced acumen and insight when it came to speaking to and dating girls.

I absorbed and learned from my family's entrepreneurial spirits. I would attempt to sell lemonade, baked goods, or drawings I had made to the customers. Often, somebody would be generous towards me and reward my efforts. Enough money was made to keep me interested in trying my hand in sales. The women and the shop, in general, were supportive of my efforts to earn money from doing things around the beauty salon. My Grandma Sarah would always pay me to wash the storefront windows or take out the trash.

I found creative ways to make pocket-change before ever having a real job. When a customer was finished with drinking a soda, I would request to take the can and joyfully jumped on the can outside the shop. Once it was crushed, I would throw it in a black plastic garbage bag. When I had filled enough bags, I would take them in for cash. I would collect the soda cans I gathered and turn them into the recycling center for money. I purchased a Can Crusher with the first money I earned from collecting cans. This made my business more streamlined and profitable. I could get more cans in each bag, thus increasing the amount of weight and money I could earn. My funds increased and I likely spent the money on action figures or snacks from the store. As a kid, I still remember how awesome it was to go into the store and buy whatever my heart desired.

Having a Mom as a beautician afforded my siblings and me the benefit of free hair styling. One time, my brothers and I wanted braids like the rap group members of Kris Kross. They were a popular group when we were growing up as kids. We did not have enough hair for braids, but when our hair grew long enough, my mom put extensions in our hair. The extensions were cool and the style change was noticed at school. However, they would fall out on the playground and they became not so cool to have. I guess you can call it a phase, but I preferred them over my Mom's haircuts. If we couldn't get to a barber, my Mother would experiment with cutting our hair. She did her best, but I ended up with a few 'Najees' myself. If we were lucky, my brothers and I would get haircuts from our skilled cousins or at The Barber College.

After certain hair trends faded, my brothers and I wanted waves in our hair. My brothers had smoother hair than me, so Tera gave me a texturizer to help condition and lay down my hair. The treatment was successful and soon after I was able to get the waves in my hair. The secret to getting waves is to brush your hair constantly, wetting your hair slightly when applying the wave grease, and wearing a wave cap at night. At that age, boys were having competitions to see who could have the most waves around their heads. Needless to say, we took full advantage of the expertise within our family for hair.

My father was a barber amongst many other things, but that is the job I remember him having most when I was a kid. When he was living in Cincinnati, he worked at a local barbershop called Lou's. My brothers and I would go and visit him there on the weekends and get haircuts from Dad. I sometimes would play chess with the owner, Mr. Lou. He cut me no slack on the sixty-four squares of war. One time, I made the mistake of letting him cut my hair when my Dad wasn't there. He messed my hairline up so bad that it caused a cowlick in the front of my head. I realize now he was drunk when he cut my hair. He had my head cocked to the side and was talking about, "Yea, that's straight." Mr. Lou's haircut was my payback for the Najee massacre.

Hair has played a major role in my upbringing and I am grateful for the opportunity to have learned in that environment. It was learning lasting lessons in socializing, business, and self-efficacy. I appreciate cosmetology as an art, which is definitely therapeutic for many people. Some would say that it makes you feel good on the inside when you're looking good on the outside. I'm not sure it's that simple, but I will always remember how empowered the ladies felt exiting the shop. The customers would get their hair done and leave feeling energized and refreshed to face the world. I have a lot of respect for the professions of my Grandma Sarah, my Mother, my Dad, and Tera. I got a chance to see up close and personal how something as simple as getting your hair done could positively impact your life. Beauty and Glamour was a major component of my upbringing. God used the business and the people within it to reach me and teach me significant lessons in life.

Eric Pierre Isaacs, Regina (Fasho) Isaacs

Chapter 9

The Bully

*"And not only so, but we glory in tribulations also: knowing that tribulation worketh patience; And patience, experience; and experience, hope: And hope maketh not ashamed; because the love of God is shed abroad in our hearts by the Holy Ghost which is given unto us." **Romans 5:3-5***

The legends of bullies are myths until you encounter them for yourself. My exposure to them surprisingly started as a friendship. My childhood bully was named Chris, but in the neighborhood, he went by the nickname "T-man." He lived in the same housing projects as I called Hawaiian Village.

The neighborhood where my family lived, also known as HV, was located on a dead-end street. It bordered Colerain, which is one of the longest streets in the city of Cincinnati. At the top of the hill, there was a bus stop, where a short wooden fence was posted. T-man lived near the top of the hill. His apartment was located by the L, which was notoriously the most dangerous part of the neighborhood. The "L" had earned its name and reputation due to the design of the parking lot that leads to an isolated set of hidden apartments. The parking lot set off to the right-hand side of once in the valley of the first hill. At the bottom of the first hill, there was also a back trail through the woods that could easily be used to access the rear of the townhouses. The majority of the complexes in the neighborhood were townhouses, but the L was section eight housing for as long as I can remember.

Throughout my childhood, T-Man and I were cool and familiar with one another. We went to Mt. Airy elementary school together from third to fifth grade. Chris joined my classroom during my fifth-grade year after failing to pass the year prior. Chris was funny, and I couldn't resist being entertained by his care-free behaviour and amusing classroom antics. Chris was hilarious with jokes, had exceptional comedic time, and was the most feared student in the class. He would often use profanity fluidly too, which made him seem much tougher than he was. T-man made it known he was ready to fight anytime and he would curse aloud to make his points clear. He always got away with cursing like a sailor and had clout in the neighborhood for being someone you didn't want to mess with. He wasn't much bigger than me and we had similar body types, yet his reputation made him seem enormous.

Upon joining our classroom, he instantly established that he was a challenger for the alpha male spot. We played during recess and engaged in the normal playground mischief. We competed in sports, but Chris could not dominate me in any of the games we played. After some time, T-man became frustrated with the attention I received and began to not like me anymore. Chris would harass and 'pick' on me for no apparent reason at all. I grew to believe and recognize it as jealousy, but at the time, I was afraid of him. Looking back, Chris had plenty of reasons not to like me. I was a handsome, smart, athletic, and well-liked student in the classroom.

The change in our friendship upset me and it was hard to deal with emotionally. I tried talking to my Mother about my schoolyard dilemma and she advised me on how to handle the situation. She declared, "People are always going to be jealous of you and hate on you; how are you going to deal with it?" I listened to the advice, but at the time, the guidance was not helpful. She also instructed, "You are not allowed to hit anyone first, but if someone hits you, you have the right to defend yourself." I was not fond of the idea of letting someone get the first lick and take an obvious advantage over me. I still complied with my mother's orders. I did my best to work out problems and avoid any physical conflicts.

One day, T-Man had been harassing me and even threatened to hurt me. He told the whole class that he was going to beat me up when I got off the school bus. I experienced anxiety and was worried the entire day during school. My mind was distracted by what was bound to happen once the final school bell had rung. I watched the clock throughout the day and anguished with each passing minute.

At the end of the day, I remember feeling like butterflies were flying around in my stomach. Any other time, I would have rushed to the back of the bus where all the so-called cool kids would sit. However, on this particular day, things were much different. I distinctly remember sitting towards the front of the bus that day, right next to the bus driver. I tried to spark up small conversations with the bus driver in the hopes that he might save me when that dreaded time came. I had never held a conversation with him before, but on this day, I was seeking an ally. It's times like these you find the unlikeliest allies. The driver looked at me curiously, trying to figure out why I was so interested in talking to him all of a sudden. On the ride home, I became increasingly nervous and fearful as we neared closer to my bus stop. My young mind could not help but to imagine horrible scenarios of what could occur.

As we approached Hawaiian Village, I noticed that T-Man was already there eagerly waiting for my arrival. He had left school early that day and walked home, so he had time to prepare himself for the 'beat-down' he planned to give me. He also had time to rally support from his friends and the neighborhood kids. Not only was he there, but so was a large crowd of spectators and a group of boys posted on bicycles. The crowd cheered and roared enthusiastically as the bus approached the stop. The kids were excited to see the drama unfold and possible bloodshed.

I looked at the bus driver to see if he noticed the lynch mob there waiting on me to exit. I pleaded with him and asked, "Aren't you going to help me?" The unconcerned driver looked back at me and said, "Hey man, I got other stops to make, so you have to get off the bus." I braced myself for what was about to come. At first, I hesitated to get off the bus. The bus driver insisted that it was time for me to get off. I couldn't exactly interpret all the words and yelling being directed towards me, but the crowd was urging T-Man to start the rumble. The bus driver opened the door and said to me again, "Come on, man, you have to get off the bus!" I had not thought about a plan for what I would do if the bus driver would not help me. My mind was racing a hundred miles an hour, trying to figure out what my next move was going to be. In an instance, I discovered the best course of action was evasion. I quickly devised a plan to run home for refuge as fast as I could.

All of a sudden, I quickly darted off the school bus. I used my athleticism to skip and juke right past the angry mob. I was operating on pure adrenaline, so I gained ten feet of distance before T-man and his goons decided to chase me. Even though the boys were riding bikes, they had a hard time tracking me down. As I ran for my life, my heartbeat pounded through my chest with every stride. Once I made it down the first hill, I knew that there was a chance for me to make it home safely. I quickly ran through the back trail in the woods. With the boys on bikes, it would have been impossible for them to follow me through the rugged terrain. The mini bike-gang and T-

Man had no choice but to take the long way down the hill. This allowed me enough time to evade temporarily. I remember fumbling through my keys as I rushed to open the front door of my townhouse.

I crossed the threshold, locked the door, and immediately began to feel some relief. I bent over with my hands on my knees, as I was gasping for air, trying to recover and catch my breath. At the time, I had no idea that my sister Tera was already home. She unexpectedly came around the corner in her robe, while eating a bowl of cereal with no milk per her usual. In a very calm voice, she began to investigate by asking me, "Why are you so out of breath?" I tried to pretend like I was out of oxygen and could not respond. The only words I could get out were, "I was running." She questioned me again by asking with further concern, "So, what are you running from?" I began to utter an excuse and continue to act like I was too exhausted to respond. Soon after, my explanation was overshadowed by an overwhelming noise that could be heard from outside of our home. The crowd noise was loud enough to intrigue my sister to gander outside through the window blinds for herself. With her cereal in her left hand, she used the right hand and pulled down the blinds to see what was causing the uproar.

The group of kids were yelling and demanding that I come outside and fight. Hence, she closed the blinds and asked me quite frankly, "Are you running from them?" I'm sure that my sister already knew the answer to her question, but I continued to act like I was completely out of breath and could not respond. I continued to take deep inhales and exhales in an attempt to buy myself some time and sympathy. Suddenly, my sister escorted me to the front door and opened it. She looked at me and said, "It's time to stop running; Kick his ass!" Next, she shoved me forcefully out of the door and locked it behind me. Running away or peacefully resolving the issue were no longer options for me. I was in shock, but beyond all fear and doubt, I was going to finally face my bully once and for all. This was the moment of truth!

The first time we fought, I did not give my very best effort. I was in a defensive mode just trying to do everything I could to avoid taking any big shots. However, I did recognize during the scuffle that T-man was not able to overpower me or land any punches that did any major damage. His bark was much bigger than his bite. Once he got one good shot in and a reaction from the crowd, T-Man was satisfied with the results and no longer desired to fight. The outcome of the battle was essentially a draw, with Chris getting in one solid punch in the brawl. I was just happy the incident was over, or at least I thought it was.

After the fight, I knocked on my front door anticipating what my sister would say. She calmly opened the door and asked me, "Did you kick his ass?" In embarrassment, I hung my head and shook it side to side indicating 'No'. Tera's eyes grew bigger as we made eye contact and I looked at her in embarrassment. She made sure she had my undivided attention before speaking further. With a serious gaze, she looked at me and said, "Well, this time if you don't kick his ass, I'm going to kick your ass!" For as much as I was afraid of T-man, I was much more afraid of my heavy-handed sister. Tera punched like a man and she was the closest thing I had to a father figure for many years of my childhood. As a kid, I feared Tera's wrath more than my mother or anybody else on Earth.

My sister once again sent me outside to fight and locked the door behind me. The crowd was still scarcely gathered in front of my townhouse. People were laughing and recapping what had just occurred. I caught up with T-man and challenged him to another round. He replied, "Oh you want some more of this?" I countered by saying, "It's not over!" This made the crowd assemble once again as they anxiously anticipated the rematch. Everyone in attendance was likely expecting T-Man to easily earn another victory.

The first time we fought, I was afraid of T-Man's aggressive words and his reputation in the neighborhood. The second time around, I embraced the fact that he could not physically dominate me. I was more of the aggressor and instantly grappled Chris, so he could not throw any punches at me. My wrestling instincts started to kick in once we were locked in a clinch. I gained body control over the action and used it to exert myself. I was able to toss him around much more than he was able to stop me. The scrap eventually led us to rumble on the ground. In the tussle, T-Man was able to free one arm and deliver a strike to my face. He looked confused as I was unfazed by the punch and immediately returned the lick. Once I was mounted in the top position, the crowd broke up the fight. I definitely got the upper hand in the second contest.

I left that skirmish with my confidence and no longer afraid of the big bad T-Man. I went back to the house and knocked on the door. My sister kindly asked me again, "Did you kick his ass?" This time, with a half-smile on my face, I shook my head up and down with dignity. My sister then opened the door wide and embraced me with a hug. Finally, I felt some relief from having to face my fear. I thank God for my sister's presence and timely intervention at this critical point in my life.

After that fight, Chris had a lot more respect for me and left me alone in class. I always thought of him as a friend anyway, so it was nice to move past this roadblock in my life. Facing the bully was a valuable life lesson and a necessary evil of my life's journey. T-man and I returned to a friendship based on mutual respect and laughter. I encountered Chris several times as we grew up. My family eventually moved to a house in a different neighborhood. Once I started driving, I would sometimes go to Hawaiian Village and visit T-Man. Even then, he looked like he wanted to challenge me to another match. However, I'm sure he thought twice about it every time.

Sadly, Chris passed away at the young age of twenty-five from Lupus. I don't look at my bully experience like most people might. My bully was a likable guy who I had a lot of admiration for. He was not daunting in stature or hovering over me in some massive domineering way. We were similar in body types and he was an evenly matched opponent for me. The experience, as a whole, played a significant role in the formation of the man I am today. Chris toughened me up and helped me realize my ability to defend myself. My heavenly father was teaching me that thou shall not fear. I am thankful for T-Man's life because through it God taught me a lesson in manhood and I haven't run from anything since. We can only run from trouble or problems for so long. There are times in life when men, and even boys, are called to show some courage and faith.

Fear thou not; for I am with thee: be not dismayed; for I am thy God: I will strengthen thee; yea, I will help thee; yea, I will uphold thee with the right hand of my righteousness." **Isaiah 41:10**

Illustrated by Davide Dart Rota

Chapter 10

All In

"I can do all things through Christ which strengthens me."
Philippians 4:13

For as long as I can remember, I have always been physically active and enjoyed playing sports. I was a natural athlete and very active outside during my youth. I played sports daily in the neighborhood and seasonally for organized teams. The sports I played routinely were football, basketball, baseball, and golf. I played one of those sports with each season of the year; Football during the fall, basketball during the winter, baseball during the spring, and golf during the summer.

The first extracurricular activity that I actually participated in was karate. When my older sister was a teen, she was a counselor for a summer program that I attended. The building next to this facility is where the karate lessons were given. I would see them practicing when we were exiting the summer program for the day. I remember feeling the excitement from the action as I glared through the large window in the front of the building with intrigue.

Shortly after that, I asked my Mother if I could receive karate lessons near the camp and grudgingly she said yes. She had no issue with me wanting to try something new and be involved in the community, but as a single mother, she recognized that she would have to finance my adventure. The financial requirement for my participation was new for my Mom, but she budgeted and made sure I had everything I needed. I walked into my first lesson with my registration fee paid and a freshly pressed white Gi and belt to boot. I was nervous at first, but I learned to enjoy the mental and physical development and training.

The instructors were two bald-headed men of average size, but you could tell by the look on their faces that they meant business. They looked tough and demanded discipline and obedience from each kid participating. These men served as positive male role models for me early on in my life. They showed me how to work hard, follow direct instructions, and be disciplined in my actions. These men invested in my mind and body, and it helped me build confidence, integrity, and self-esteem. My body began to spurt as I grew taller and stronger than many of my peers. I recall developing immensely between the ages of nine and ten.

I can still remember the first karate tournament I ever competed in. I was so nervous and unsure of my abilities. I had no awareness about what was going on or what was bound to occur. The stands were filled with people and there were several individuals gathered on the mats as well. There were tables set up, where highly ranked individuals would sit and critique each contestant. The atmosphere was amazing and I observed the many matches, forms competitions, and judge tables. This first tournament was a blur to me competitively.

At the tournament, we were evaluated on our knowledge of martial arts as well as our performance of our forms and fighting. I was stimulated and learning from the environment and experience of the competition. For me, that tournament was overshadowed by my disbelief in what I could do at the time. I ended up placing fourth place overall in fighting and forms and the prize was a nice wooden plaque. I felt some accomplishment from not leaving empty-handed, but I was still unaware of the power and strength that dwelled within.

My Mother was not very impressed or happy with the results of the first tournament. I told her what happened and she must have sensed that I had held back in my abilities at the tournament or under-appreciated her funds. She paid money for me to compete in the tournament and from her perspective, I came home with a piece of wood. My Mom yelled at me about not having the money to pay for "these-extra" tournament fees, especially if I was only going to bring home a piece of wood, and not try to win it all. I took her comments seriously and realized I was in danger of losing something I had grown to enjoy. My Mother set the standard and I accepted the challenge to continue participating in karate. She told me, "If you don't bring something home from the next tournament, it will be your last one!"

My Mom was fine with me playing any sport I wanted to - It was a positive way of keeping me out of trouble and out of the streets - I can't recall her being present at any tournaments or games. In fact, I can only remember her attending two games the entire time I participated in sports. One of those times, my Mom came to a baseball game with my Godmother, Charlene, and Creester. The second time was when she came to a football game during my high school playing days. The other kids had parents and family members at each and every sporting event. With no parent there to root for me, I had to find an internal reason to rise to the occasion. However, my Mom never stopped me from playing any sport and she made sure I could participate. I appreciate that she always supported me financially for recreational sports.

The following karate tournament, I put my fears and worries aside and gave it my best. My Stepdad drove me out to the

Tri-County area where the tournament was being held in a hotel. I embraced the support and encouragement I received from my team. This time around, I was engaged in the environment and realized that I was there to compete. I searched around for possible opponents and practiced moves to counter moves they were demonstrating. I was all in and ready to fight for my opportunity to continue doing that which I loved. By the end of the tournament, I had placed second in fighting and third place in forms. I gave it my best and I was satisfied with the result and performance. It required some courage and bravery, but I was able to get the job done by believing in God and myself. To my surprise, the trophies I earned in that tournament were a considerable upgrade from the wooden plaque. The reward was two large, shiny, gold-plated trophies. The second-place trophy measured half the size of my body and the third-place trophy was about two feet tall. I could barely carry them to the car when it was time to go.

My Stepdad picked me up from the tournament, helped me load them into the car, and then drove me to my Mother's beauty salon. I remember feeling excited as I exited the car and headed towards the door of my Mothers' place of business. I first saw my Grandma Sarah's smile as she alerted my Mother to my arrival. My Mother ran out the door cheering and celebrating as I approached with the large trophies in both hands. She approved of the harvest I brought back.

I felt so proud of my accomplishments that day. I made my Mother proud, but I learned a much more valuable life lesson. The whole experience became a vital part of my character formation. I have grown to know that I perform the best when my back is against the wall. I have learned that when people count me out, underestimate me, or focus too much on my failures, it prompts and motivates me to prove them wrong. Some people might refer to this phenomenon as resilience; the ability to achieve when the odds are stacked against you. I have learned that it has more to do with faith and tapping into the greatness of God in everything we do. Moving forward, I grew an appreciation for competing and challenging myself to be my best.

"Not only that, but we rejoice in our sufferings, knowing that suffering produces endurance, and endurance produces character, and character produces hope, and hope does not put us to shame, because God's love has been poured into our hearts through the Holy Spirit who has been given to us." **Romans 5:3-5**

Around the age of nine, we moved from Bahama Terrace to Hawaiian Village. There were many more kids around due to it being a much larger neighborhood housing. My townhouse was a three-story building with plenty of space for my family. We needed more space with my brother Rico on his way to stay at home. Downstairs there was a family room and my sister Tera's room was in a large utility room with the washer and dryer. She enjoyed the privacy of being the only bedroom on the bottom floor and the access she had to a door. This meant she didn't need to sneak into the house if she ever missed curfew. Up one flight of stairs was the dining room leading to a balcony door. The kitchen was to the left of the balcony. Also on that floor was a half bathroom and the living room. Up another set of stairs were three bedrooms and a full bathroom. The townhouses were rather nice, especially for low to middle-income large families.

I remember looking out of the window as a young boy watching the older boys in the neighborhood as they socialized and gathered each weekend in front of my house. I was not certain of what was going on, but later I learned that they were picking teams. The games were held on the hilly patch of grass that stretched the length of my complex. Once the teams were chosen, they eventually began to play football. I watched and admired them from my window noticing the moves, skills, and rules of the game. It was a contact sport, so I was easily attracted to the masculine and machismo attitude and behavior associated with it. This was my first real exposure to the sport and how boys congregated to play and compete within the neighborhood.

The second time I saw them out there, I went outside to investigate how I could play and get into the game. It was exciting just to mingle among my peers and the older boys. I was quickly shut down and told "No" because I was too small to play. However, I did not let the initial rejection discourage me from trying. I sat on the sidelines and watched and learned from the big boys how to play the game. I paid attention to which moments and moves would cause the most crowd noise. I would practice many of the skills and techniques that I would see them doing outside. I used a water bottle to work on my hand and eye coordination before I had a football. I would use anything near me that could be used to improve my catching. I learned quickly from watching the big boys, reading books, and watching any football game I could catch on television.

The following week, just like clockwork, the boys were in front of my house playing football again. I wondered with excitement if this would be the day I would be able to make my mark on the field and among the neighborhood boys. I asked to play, but once again I was told no because I was too small to play. This time, the word came down from Zareef, who was a skinny high school age guy with huge lips and a large afro. In defense of sure jokes he would face in life, Zareef became an excellent roaster and comedian. He was known in the neighborhood to be the funniest "capper" and was very witty with his comebacks. Due to his prowess and clout, Zareef earned respect in the neighborhood among the other kids.

After the game, I went up to Zareef and asked him, *"Why wouldn't you let me play?"* He returned, "because you can't hit Lil Nigga!" I looked him directly in his face and expressed to him, "*I can hit you!*" This got a few gasps from other kids that were standing nearby. Zareef was not about to be embarrassed or shown up by some younger kid. He instantly accepted the challenge and demanded the nearby football, so he could in his words, "Run this Lil Nigga over!" He informed me, "We are going to go heads up!" I was unsure of what that was so I questioned, "*What is that?*" Zareef replied, "I am going to run the ball and you're going to hit me like you said you can do!" He continued by swearing, "I'm going to run your little ass over!"

I braced myself for the overwhelming odds and impact soon to come. He voiced out, "Set, Go" and came running forward towards me. I came forward as well and hit him with my shoulder while wrapping my arms around his skinny waist and legs. I halted his progress, however, he began to painfully dig and ram his razor-sharp knees into my chest. I was holding on for dear life and determined not to let go. I remember holding on so tightly to lessen the blow I would receive from every stride. I was not able to take him down, but he did not run me over either. I remember feeling some pain, but I pretended to conceal the hurt. He asked me if I was okay and my response was yes as he walked away to catch up with his friends.

The following Sunday when it was time for the boys to play football, I was already outside prior to them arriving. I was practicing on the side as they congregated to decide on teams. I waited on the sideline anxiously anticipating and looking for an opportunity to play. My hopes waned as it came closer to the end of picking teams. On the final pick, the big boys were debating on which person to select. They were looking around to see if anybody else left could be used to help their team. Suddenly, Zareef advocated for me to be picked because he asserted that, "A, he can hit!" I was picked for the game and this honestly started my love for the game of football. Finally, I had earned the respect of one of the big boys in the neighborhood.

I felt accepted as I was picked to play in several games after that.

My best friend growing up in Hawaiian Terrace was my next-door neighbor, Alex. However, the first person I met and became good friends with was a short, fast, and popular kid from the neighborhood named Shane. He was allowed to play in the neighborhood games too and he played organized sports for a team. He is the reason I even found out about where the organized football team was practicing. Consequently, I followed him to the Hilltop Hawks. Another kid from my neighborhood that played on my teams was named Troy. He lived up the street from me, and we could always hear his mom calling him home. Chorally, she would call out, "Trooooooyyyyyyy!" We thought it was funny as kids. Troy had an outstanding arm and was an exceptional basketball player and quarterback. To many of us growing up, he was the next thing closest to Michael Jordan. Troy was an exceptional athletic ability for his age and could dunk, dribble, and shoot much ahead of his time. He threw the tightest spiral as a quarterback as well.

Shane and I were the same age, so we played together on many of the same teams. Being friends with him led me to find a baseball and basketball team to join. I loved my experiences in youth football with the Hilltop Hawks. Each age level in the organization had a different type of name, with the word hawks included in it. For example, there were the Seahawks, Nighthawks, Mini-Hawks, and Red Hawks, and so on. There, I met a few people that are still a part of my life today. I have learned that once you are on a team with someone, sometimes, they become your teammates for life.

Most of my first year of playing organized football was fast-paced and hazy memory, but I remember learning the fundamentals and pacing of the game. I understood the basic concepts of the game, however, I did not know how to apply them to their highest potential just yet. I still soaked up any information or skills that were made available to me. Several black men served as my coaches and many of these men became positive role models in my life. Growing up without my father, I vastly appreciated how these men contributed to me realizing that my best was good enough.

The head coach of the Hilltop Hawks was named Coach Joe. He was not at every practice, but he was at each game and we knew that he was the head coach. He would always advocate for our team on the sidelines and argue with the referees proclaiming, "That's bullshit!" Several of the football players thought his ranting was entertaining. Shane and I jokingly mocked him saying, "That's bullshit!" whenever we thought it would be funny. Coach Joe's signature phrase, however, was "Stop loafing!" Loafing was when someone was not trying hard or giving their best effort. As kids, we thought his sayings were hilarious and all the players joked about them outside of practice. Even during practice, we would tell each other to stop loafing when we were looking for a laugh. Some of the players did not like Coach Joe because his coaching did not lead us to a Super Bowl. He was more of a disciplinarian and authoritarian than he was a motivating and technical coach. For a kid from a fatherless home though, his presence as a coach still communicated to me that he cared.

Coach Ed was the Offensive Coordinator and he was a lot more technical about what he wanted from us as players. He was a shorter guy, and he would always wear his skullcaps rolled upon his head. Many of the players thought this was also funny, but we loved him as our coach. His son, Marcus, became one of my better friends throughout my childhood years. I remember spending time at his house playing basketball or whatever sport was in season at that time. I would also just go over to play video games and hang out with Marcus. Coach Ed was also the baseball coach for the neighborhood Hilltop team and my age group. He set a standard and expected us to be able to fulfill it to the best of our abilities. He was encouraging and consistent with the offense and that was very much appreciated. He was a great athlete himself and would display his talent at times in practice if requested unanimously by the players. He recognized my talents and abilities much before I ever knew they existed. He noticed my aggressiveness and good hands, so he groomed me into a starting tight end.

Coach Jimmy was responsible for the defensive line and offensive line. He was a tall, dark-skinned man with glasses, a beard, and a deep voice. He was the main coach that was responsible for getting me ready to play defensively. He would practice me in drills repetitiously and be very encouraging, motivating, and patient with me. He was one of my favorite coaches of all time because he truly believed in me. Being the developmental coach, Coach Jimmy took my athleticism and showed me how to use it to help my team. His wife, Mrs. Pat, had a gold tooth in front of her mouth and ran an all-purpose business out of her van. She sold any and all football equipment one might be looking for as well as team apparel. She had a profitable business and competed with many of the local vendors. I didn't know, but Coach Jimmy and Mrs. Pat were the presidents of the Hilltop Hawks during my childhood.

Coach Malone was another one of my coaches who had a son on the team. His son was named Dominic and his mother was the Team Mom. I remember going to watch Coach Malone himself play and see him just clobber people on the football field. He was a massive middle linebacker and had a tough personality and nasty demeanor about him. He urged players to be aggressive, bend the rules, and to leave all of their energy out on the field. He mainly worked on the defensive side of the ball whenever he was active with the team. He once told me on the field, "If you ain't cheating, you ain't trying hard enough!" It was probably bad advice, but I deciphered what he meant.

He was instructing us players to give our all and then give some more.

Another tough coach I had was Coach Darnell. He would cuss and call out players if we were underachieving or under-performing. He had a son on the team named Darnell as well. Coach Darnell was a medium-sized, stocky built man with a goatee and several gold teeth. He had no problem using profanity when he felt it was necessary because of our play. I remember one game we were down in points to a football team called Western AA. We had historically beaten the team, but this year the Warriors had a white quarterback at the time. He was running freely against our defense and scored a couple of touchdowns in the first half. At half time, Coach Darnell tore into us screaming, "What the fuck are y'all doing? Y'all are letting Forrest Gump run all over y'all asses!" He was a tough-minded no-nonsense type of coach, but he was at least present at critical points of my life. I at least knew that he was on my side, no matter how mean he was.

Coach Hosea or "Coach Ball" was also a yeller and had an aggressive, yet encouraging style of coaching and personality. His son, Hosea, had hazel eyes and was our running back and defensive back. Coach Ball rarely missed a practice and was a constant male figure during my days playing youth sports. Coach Richardson was a dad, but he helped with the team at times as well. All of these coaches did their part in teaching me the finer points of the game of football and life. Coach Ed, Coach Hosea, and Coach Richardson were all cousins. Coach Richardson's son, Dwight, was our star athlete and team captain. He was our leader, our enforcer, and an outstanding athlete in all sports. The Clark, Cannon, and Richardson boys were the core of our team. They had an uncle named Vinny, who played for Ohio State and then professional football in the NFL.

Last but not least, was Coach Clarence. He worked with the offense because his son Chris was the quarterback for my team. Everybody within the organization called Chris "Rocky". Coach Clarence was the basketball coach for the Hilltop Hawks, but he was involved with the football team at times throughout my childhood. He and his wife were Detectives for the Cincinnati Police Department. Coach Clarence was a classy gentleman, and yet another positive black male I became familiar with growing up.

Shane, Marcus, Hosea, Dwight, Dominic, Darnell, and I played multiple sports together throughout the year, so we had a camaraderie. This early brotherhood assisted me in my development as a youth. I spent countless hours with these boys competing and practicing during critical years of my development. I played hard for my team, so I was always received well and respected by my teammates.

Unfortunately, my association with the football team also included me experiencing the death of someone on the team. Gabe was one of the best running backs to ever play for our football team. I remember he would always wear duct tape around his thigh pads for each game. When asked why he did it, Gabe responded by saying, "It made him faster!" His output during the games was undeniable, so the duct tape for him was highly effective and became his signature mark. He was sadly killed in a drug-related incident when we were close to being teenagers. Gabe was a good kid and stellar athlete, but he was also active in the streets in his time away from the team. His funeral was the first one I went to that involved someone I really knew. I can still picture the sobbing kids and adults at his casket. I remember looking at his lifeless body as he laid in peace. By the age of twelve, the reality of death could no longer evade the innocence of my mind.

As it is, there are many parts, but one body. The eye cannot say to the hand, "I don't need you!" And the head cannot say to the feet, "I don't need you!" On the contrary, those parts of the body that seem to be weaker are indispensable, and the parts that we think are less honorable we treat with special honor. And the parts that are unpresentable are treated with special modesty, while our presentable parts need no special treatment. But God has put the body together, giving greater honor to the parts that lacked it, so that there should be no division in the body, but that its parts should have equal concern for each other. **1 Corinthians 12:20-25**

During my first year playing football, I remember getting in a few games towards the end of the games, which we were ahead in. Those plays still seem like a blur to me, but it was a necessary experience in order to gain the necessary football intelligence. I needed to learn how to play the game on an organized level first. By my second year, I had figured out how to use all the skills from practice and the moves I honed the neighborhood. My ten-year-old year was my glory year for me playing youth sports. My girlfriend at the time was the Captain of the cheerleading team for my age group. The time spent on the field, with the team, and the coaches allowed me to feel assured in myself.

I had continued to sprout and earned starting positions on offense, defense, and special teams. For the overwhelming majority of my days of playing organized football, I played outside linebacker, tight end, and punter. If I wasn't punting the ball, I was normally the long snapper for the punter. I stayed on the field in all phases of the game and contributed positively to my team.

Coach Eddie had noticed my improved abilities during try-outs and started to groom me at tight end. I was extremely fast due to my conditioning, so Coach Ed designed a play to get me the ball called the "end and around." We ran the play often in games and I scored 10 touchdowns on offense during my ten-year-old season. There were a few games where I had two touchdowns in the same game. From that time forward, I became a critical part of our team on offense and defense. I enjoyed all the sports I engaged in, but football was probably my favorite to play. I can still smell the dew on the grass in the early morning on football grass. I remember the smell of the hamburgers steaming from the grill near the concessions tent. I can still feel the butterflies that would float in my stomach from nervousness prior to the games. I learned that the only remedy for the butterflies was my first contact. I made a point to get a hit early in the game to get rid of them. I vividly remember turning the corners and out-running every player on the football field to the touchdown.

Around the age of 12, many of the kids on the Hilltop Hawks started playing sports for the middle schools they attended. Some kids continued to play in the recreational league, but most of the players decided to pursue greener pastures playing school ball. A few teammates and I went and played youth football with the Avondale Warriors. The coaches there were horrible coaches and they had no idea how to use me on the football field. They rarely used me on defense or offense. When I did get in they would split me out so far outside to draw a defender away from the play. This was a wasted use of my talents and a year of football, but my love for the game remained the same.

Going to Walnut Hills High School, my Mother was more concerned with me doing well academically, so she did not let me play sports in high school until my sophomore year. I finally tried out for the football team during my junior year. I kind of hesitated because I had believed that all of the positions were already spoken for by previous upperclassmen. We had a dominant senior class of players and many of the people on the team were returning players who had been playing for several years. A few students who were also former Hilltop Hawks informed me that they were going out for the team. One of them was already a member and had been trying to convince me and other Hawks that there were opportunities for spots on the team. I was also driving by this time, so it became a convenient way for me and my pals to get to practice.

I showed up for practice and it was just as I had feared. Many of the positions were already occupied, including my traditional position of defensive end/outside linebacker. My natural spot was filled by a senior named Clinton, who was also a star running back, baseball player, and athlete in the school. There was an open spot at cornerback, so I first thought it would be a good idea to try out for cornerback. I had never played the position in the past, but my brother played cornerback, so I was familiar with it and knew the basic requirements. I was an athlete and able to do most of the drills without error, but I did not stand out at the position because it was not meant for me.

I became what was referred to as a "Chinese Bandits" or Junior Varsity. The Chinese Bandits were used to prepare the varsity squad for their upcoming opponents. As a bandit, you basically could expect pain and punishment, as the varsity did their best to trample over you and make an example. My football abilities started to speak for themselves and I quickly began to outgrow the bandits. I was leveling other kids in practice and especially during Junior Varsity games. On JV, I got a chance to play with a few old friends from Hilltop, like Jay, our quarterback. He and I connected on several pass plays and long runs during our time playing together. I would happily throw hellacious blocks for Jay when he scrambled, setting him free to run. I had some crushing hits on opponents and it wasn't long before Coach Sharp relayed the information to Coach Young. I overheard him say, "You have to get Isaacs off

JV before someone gets hurt." As a player, I appreciated his recommendation and confirmation.

The first high school varsity game I participated in was against Harrison and I did not play one single play in the game. I became frustrated because I had success against Harrison's teams at the youth level. I remember watching the game and thinking that Harrison wasn't doing anything that I could not handle or stop. This was the first game that I had ever rode the bench. My team lost and it disturbed me to my core that I did not spend one play on the field helping the team. I headed to the bus upsettingly after shaking hands at the end of the game. I saw our Coach, John Young, standing outside the bus smoking a cigarette. My spirit led me to walk right up to him and exclaimed, "*Coach Young, this is the first time ever that I have not gotten into a game, and it bothers me to see us lose and I'm not on the field to help my team.*" He pondered on what I said to him as he took a couple of deep drags his cigarette, "SSSSuuuuu, Wheeeeew, you know what Eric Isaacs, you're absolutely right, we are going to find somewhere to put you on the field!" I was thrilled, eager, and ready for the chance to earn my rightful spot on the varsity football team.

The following week in practice, Coach Young escorted me from the cornerbacks to where the linebackers were practicing. He urged, "Come on over here Eric Isaacs, I want you to get to learn this outside linebacker position." Little did he know, I had been playing that spot my entire life. It did not take long for my abilities at the position to shine and for the coaches to notice my potential. Coach Young also made the decision to put me on the kick-off team on special teams for the upcoming game.

The following contest was against Turpin and I got a total of two plays during that game. However, I made each of them count for two tackles, including one being a forced fumble. On the first kickoff, I sped down the field in my lane as I was coached to do. I continued to press forward as I took notice of how strong and big the high school players were. I was among the tacklers on that play, and it gave our team great field position. In the second kick-off, I made a tackle on the ball carrier that led to a fumble recovery. While making the tackle, I targeted the football with my helmet and was able to knock it loose. My coaches noticed my effort on those plays and the team started to give me praise for my contributions on the football field. I put on a dominant performance on offense and defense during the JV game the following day. By this time, I had generated plenty of buzz among the players and coaches as an instinctive hard-hitting football player who could help the team.

The next game was our homecoming game against Purcell Marian. It was the most important game on our schedule too many of the coaches and players because of a neighborhood rivalry. The stands were packed with alumni, fans, and students. There were so many people there that some had to wrap around the track of the field in order to see the game. From the start of the game, Clint was having issues containing his side and making the necessary tackles at outside linebacker. He made a few big errors early in the game, and the Defensive Coordinator, Coach Deerwater, screeched, "Eric Isaacs, get in there!" I came in the game as an outside linebacker and immediately was able to make a positive impact and contribution to the game. I had been playing the position my whole life, so I could recognize the plays before they even occurred and anticipate how to best defend the plays. I played well even with very little preparation for starting the position during the weekly practice. We ended up losing the game 21-19, but afterward, the coaches and seniors were fired up about my performance.

By the end of the game, Coach Deerwater yelled at me, "Eric Isaacs, YOU ARE NO LONGER A CHINESE BANDIT! YOU ARE NOW STARTING OUTSIDE LINEBACKER!" It was a great moment for me because from then on, the seniors accepted me as their own and took me underneath their wings. I was relieved that all of my hard work had paid off and allowed me to become the starting defensive end for my varsity high school football team.

The following game was a highly anticipated game against Woodward, which was the high school where my mother graduated. Her boyfriend at the time, Anthony, was also a graduate from Woodward and attended the game. At the time, Woodard had a quarterback who was considered a premier player in the league. I had played him previously at the youth level, each time with success in the form of victory. Coach Deerwater put in the perfect game plan for the bout. He noticed that the quarterback would often scramble and then return to the initial point of attack. He instructed the defense to fire off the line of scrimmage but to hold our positions and not chase the elusive quarterback all over the field. His plan worked to perfection and we were able to put the quarterback out of the game early. I put on a show for those attending this game by getting four sacks and my performance was even written about in the local newspaper. I didn't realize it until the captain of the football team reported, "Hey, they are blowing you up in this paper!"

At the end of the game, we were up 40-0, so our coach would substitute young players in to gain valuable playing time and experience. An underclassman named Ryan was in the game playing the opposite defensive end as myself. We both converged on the quarterback on this particular play. I was a second ahead of him and made the tackle cleanly. He happened to dive with his head down and rammed my thigh with his helmet on the missed tackle attempt. This caused a major contusion in my thigh, and I played hurt for the remainder of the year. It was painful to run and I could not use the same agility I was used to playing with.

I was limping around on crutches and was severely hampered in my walking and running ability. I was going to sit out and rest for a few games, but the senior cornerback on my side, Jamel, encouraged me to just give whatever I had left. He appealed to me, "P, I would rather have you out there on the field hurt than anybody else on that sideline." I didn't want to let him or the seniors down, so I played the remainder of the season hurt for the team. I wasn't able to dominate like before the injury, but I was able to play my position well enough for the team to continue surging. That season solidified my reputation among the players and raised the expectation for the junior class the following year. We were able to go for a run at the state tournament, but we lost our final game that year to West High.

I earned an academic scholarship from a local college due to my play during my junior year, however, it was lost due to being academically ineligible. I was so immersed in my social life and popularity that I did not take my Chemistry course as seriously as I should have. I ended up failing the class in the fourth quarter, which made me ineligible for the spring sports the upcoming year. The football scholarship was lost due to my academic performance. It definitely has been a lesson learned that I have shared with others in hopes they avoid making the same mistake. I lost sight of what was important and it cost me my senior year. I could have come back with three games left, but I was devastated by missing out on the season. I let my team down, and I wish I had the perseverance back then to come back and finish those three games and give my team a boost leading into the playoffs. Sometimes in life, you only get one chance to do things the right way.

I was a good basketball player, but not a great one. I didn't like the constant running up and down the court. However, since all the other kids on my team and in the neighborhood played basketball, I quickly tried to learn as much as I could about the sport. I was one of the only kids in the neighborhood who had a basketball rim. During that time, Hawaiian Village was a middle-class type of neighborhood. At first, many white people lived in the neighborhood, especially on the end caps of the townhouses. Those townhouses included a fireplace, so they were premier locations when we first moved in. I was at least privileged enough to receive a cool Christmas gift that made me a popular kid on the block.

Even though it was my basketball rim, the big boys would come and dominate it. They didn't pass me the ball or pick me for teams initially, even though it was my rim! I now realize that I benefited from this mentorship. When I could only dribble with my right hand, the older boys would take my right side away from me and steal the ball. There was no other choice than to develop my left hand. I would dribble to the candy lady's store or to the pool using only my left hand. I became good at grabbing rebounds, playing defense, steals, and slashing to the basket. Nobody really passed to me, so I wasn't a great shooter. I developed skills in various areas of basketball because that's how I became accustomed to playing the game. I would have to earn each and every opportunity to shoot. It was very competitive, so I did the hustle work in order to get my hands on the ball. I still had fun playing and it was yet another sport that allowed me to develop athletically and socially. I guess you could say I was Mr. Intangible.

I remember one time, my father came to see me play a game when I played for the Hilltop Hawks. It was at a gym in Avondale. I'm pretty sure the coach recognized that my father was attending this game and that I wanted to impress him. I recall that Coach Clarence put me in the game much earlier than normal that day. I played good defense and got a steal and a fast break opportunity down the court. As I ran down the court with the ball leading the pack, I was thinking about impressing my dad. My heart was pounding and I could barely control the ball or my energy in the race towards the basket. I ran as fast as possible and put up the shot. I missed the layup, but I remember my dad was still proud of me. The fact that I played good defense and got the steal did not go unnoticed. He was just happy that he got the chance to see me play. He still treated me as if I had scored 100 points.

I played basketball in middle school as well. In my seventh-grade year, I played for Heinold Foreign Language Academy. I received valuable playing minutes and scored several points for that team. I remember the highlight of the season was when I hit a faraway buzzer-beating shot. The crowd went wild! I waved my hands in a circle and then placed a hand on my ear, gesturing to hear the crowd noise like Hulk Hogan. I also played for Finneytown during my eighth-grade year and was an impactful player. I made the A squad but decided to play on the B squad for a chance to play with a close friend. Playing on the B squad also meant that I did not have to fight for minutes amongst an already crowded roster. Even though I was fairly decent at basketball, it was not my preferred sport. I was able to keep stride well enough but lost interest in high school. I enjoyed playing basketball for recreation, but not with all the non-stop running required to play it on an organized level.

To one he gave five talents, to another two, to another one, to each according to his ability. Then he went away. **Matthew 25:15**

Baseball was a different story. My brothers and sister also excelled at the sport. I learned to catch and hit the ball from my sister and in the neighborhood. I watched her and my cousin play softball for a church team. My sister was heavy-handed, so she could throw, bat, and catch with skill. My youngest brother Ricardo was a phenomenal pitcher and my handicapped brother even played as well. I remember going to his games with him and participating with him in support. During the season, we would play often with the neighborhood kids.

There were some dug out holes in the grass near the end of my complex in the shape of a baseball diamond. Home plate was backed up by a large bush, and the batter's box was on a bit of an incline. The large bush provided fodder and an automatic catcher for the times we did have enough people to have one. The pitcher's mound was on the decline of the hill, so naturally, I developed an under-hook type of swing in order to hit home runs over the patio awning past the sandbox. The end of the sandbox was considered home-run territory. To the right of the field was the woods. Many times we would have to run into the woods and retrieve the ball or find another one. We developed skills by trying to stop the ball from entering the woods or into the parking lot, where it could hit a car. I was a great outfielder in regards to catching and throwing the ball. I was good at hitting the ball deep on a consistent basis early on in my baseball days.

My main baseball coach, Coach Ed mentioned to me one time that he thought I would make a great lead-off hitter. I was a promising new baseball player, but then I went through a slump when Coach Ball tried to change my swing during a batting practice session. I missed on a pitch one time and he caught me swinging in an upward fashion. He didn't exactly show me how to do it correctly, but he yelled repeatedly, "Swing level!" I wasn't exactly sure what he was meaning by swinging level, so I started chopping at the ball rather than taking a full swing. From that time forward, my batting went into a slump for many years and I was never able to recover my natural swing. I realized later that this particular practice, the old coach may have been drunk. He had no idea the confusion he had caused in my batting motion. That just goes to show you the power of words.

"Let no corrupting talk come out of your mouths, but only such as is good for building up, as fits the occasion, that it may give grace to those who hear." **Ephesians 4:29**

After a year at Walnut Hills High School proving that I could manage my academics, my mother let me first play baseball in my sophomore year. Although my batting struggled after the experience with Coach Ball, I remained great in the outfield and at running the bases. I had a Coach in high school who was a returning player from the previous year. He took the time and showed me how to hold the bat so that I could surely make contact with the ball when I desired. Along the way, I mastered how to bunt the baseball. I learned how to control the speed and direction of the ball coming off of the bat. Bunting became a valuable weapon for me as well as my prowess in running bases. I used my base speed and knowledge of the game to get on base often. In fact, my batting average for junior varsity was .404, and more than half of my hits were bunts.

There was an art to bunting and getting on base often. I understood that you could dive to first base, but you needed to do so headfirst. I focused on being able to place and control the ball to my advantage. Every time, I could get the ball to roll down the third baseline at a very slow and deliberate pace. I would sacrifice my body and use my long arm span and solid speed to slide headfirst. In many of the games I took home scratches and scrapes from base running, but I sacrificed my body and did it happily for the team.

The last of the four sports that I played throughout my childhood years is golf. I started playing around the same time as I started playing all the other organized sports. Nine and ten years old was the time I was blooming in my development through organized sports. In Cincinnati, there was a youth golf program sponsored by a man named Tony Yates. The program had a bus that would pick us up and take us to the golf courses around the city. The pick-up and drop-off locations were in Avondale. They provided us with golf instruction, a set of basic golf clubs, transportation, and lunch as well.

It was an outstanding program to be a part of during my childhood. My brother and I both attended the golf program and became savvy golfers. In fact, three people that I went to the golf program with also attended Walnut. Golf was another sport where I showed great potential and promise. One year, I won the closest to the pin competition and earned second place in putting. I was such a great golfer at a young age. We were golfing three times a week, so we practiced often which allowed us to refine our skills. I play golf competitively, but I have always seen it as a pastime or recreational activity.

No matter what sport I was playing, I would go to my neighborhood and share the knowledge I had learned. I would practice with some of my friends or anybody who was willing to listen. I would coach many of the kids on the fundamentals of the games and allow them to use my equipment. I would also play golf with a man named Mr. T, who was a close friend of the family. He was an older guy with style, a fierce golf game, who was very easy to talk to and down to earth. He was my younger brother's Godfather, and we spent many weekends with him teaching us some of the philosophy and strategy behind the game. He would take us to Avondale Golf Course, which is a place where he won a renowned Tournament in the city of Cincinnati. He served as a positive male role model for my brother and me. There was also an older man named Mr. Gary from church, who would always talk to us about Tiger Woods, share golf knowledge, and check our grips on our golf clubs often. "A man's grip on his clubs says a lot about his grip on his life," he would always say.

Through sports, I learned the usefulness of resilience, teamwork, confidence, and discipline. I thank God for all my experiences in athletics. He has used the sports teams and the people I encountered to teach me some valuable lessons in life. A part of those lessons was figuring out how to use the abilities God gave me to overcome fear. I concluded that my doubts and concerns were not worth me not giving my all. In anything I did, I needed to be all in. I realized that "I" was enough! What God blessed me with was sufficient enough for me to excel at whatever I put my mind to. I developed a love and appreciation for the impact a positive adult male could make on a kid without being their biological father. I cherish the brotherhood of organized sports and the lessons about teamwork, life, and hard work. I thank God for using sports to keep me safely off the streets and actively engaged in something that would be positive for my path. Organized sports forced me to be accountable for the effort I put forth and the results that are put out. Ultimately, sports were used to teach me how to win and lose, honorably.

Top Left: Hosea Clark, Team Mom Malone, Troy Smith, David Sanders, Coach Jimmy, Jaman Bennett, Coach Hosea, Gabe Beckley, Coach Malone, Dwight Richardson Bottom Left: Shane Holston, Dominic Malone, Darnell Smith, Greg Carr, Eric Pierre Isaacs, Ricky Davis, Marcus Cannon

Chapter 11

Paper Chasing

"Let the wise hear and increase in learning, and the one who understands obtain guidance." Proverbs 1:5

The first school I ever attended was called Mount Airy Elementary. It still exists, however, the building has been reconstructed. I lived about two miles away from school in a neighborhood housing complex called Bahama Terrace. I remember walking to school as early as kindergarten or first grade. There were two crossing guards that would look out for students along the walk to school. Many of those guards worked the same streets each year and became familiar faces. There was an elderly black man that would always greet kids with a smile and wish them well at the first main intersection. It was a long walk for an unsupervised child to be traveling alone. I made it safely to school and back home each day. As I grew older, I went back to see the crossing guard to thank him for his service and protection during my younger years.

My kindergarten teacher's name was Miss Berry and I also had a Spanish teacher, named Señorita Hernandez. I learned my ABC's in English at the same time as I learned them in Spanish. Our kindergarten classroom was in the basement of the Mount Airy school building. I remember learning about colors, shapes, numbers, and letters in both languages. Mount Airy was a Foreign Language Academy and my mother had the insight to enroll me in the progressive academy at a young age. She knew that the Spanish language would be a major part of my future, and she was right. My childhood was heavily influenced and impacted by the Spanish culture. Many of the kids from the program ended up being in my classes as I continued throughout my educational years. In fact, three of them graduated from the same high school as I did as well.

Since an early age, I've always had a knack for making friends and talking to girls. I remember having a girlfriend as early as kindergarten. I also reminisce on the first time I ever got in trouble at school in first grade. In the classroom, I was quite talkative on most days. I was learning just as much from my social interactions as my academic ones.

One particular day, I was talking to some nearby classmates and we were indulged in a conversation. My teacher's name was Mrs. Roberts, and she was a tall, thick, white lady with a curly afro and some large glasses. Mrs. Roberts was trying to teach in front of the classroom, but my constant conversation was interfering with her teaching. I don't recall what we were talking about, but whatever it was, it had our attention and our laughing was disturbing the instruction. The teacher was frustrated and had enough of me talking out in the classroom. She suddenly stopped trying to talk over us and articulated, "Eric, shut your mouth!" Like a smart ass, I opened my mouth wide and kept it there for five seconds in opposition to her request. She was furious and I was sent to the office to see the principal. A phone call to my mother was all the discipline needed to resolve the issue.

I also remember in first grade when we were able to read, some classmates and I were standing in the back of the classroom during free time. In the rear of the class, to the far left, was the coat rack where all the jackets were hung up. Back-packs were hung there as well. To the right of that area, a large easel was located behind the student desks. A few friends and I gathered around the easel, and this girl named Blair had expressed that she had a book that her brother had given her. She was quite an advanced reader for a first grader and she began to read this book, which was about puberty and other inappropriate topics for our age. My girlfriend, Cassandra, and I pretended to act out what was being read as we snuck in kisses and hugs when we could not be seen by the teacher.

At Mount Airy, we played tetherball outside during recess time. I played on the playground often with my classmates Atiya and Courtney. I wasn't half bad at tetherball, but many of those girls were much better than I. Atiya and Courtney would use their heavy hands to whip the ball around the pole in a manner in which I couldn't compete. No matter how hard I tried it never seemed to be enough to defeat the hard-hitting girls in tetherball.

I may not have been great at tetherball, but Wall Ball was a different story. Thomas, Andre, William, Rayshon, Ned, and I would play whenever the weather permitted. There was a large wall in the rear of the school and we would throw the tennis ball against it. The person who caught the ball would earn the privilege of going up to the wall and throwing the next ball. The object of the game was to catch the ball off the wall. When the ball was bounced off the wall, everyone would position themselves to jump in the air and catch the ball. Whenever someone caught the ball while standing in front of you, it was called a "snag." We all competed and tried our best to snag one another. I was fairly tall, athletic, and could catch, so I had some epic days of wall ball during elementary school.

As we got a little older, our hormones started to rage, so during recess, we would have a baseball glove on our hands and run around touching the girls' butts. It was all consensual and in good fun. If the girls didn't want to play they simply would not run. A running girl indicated a girl who wanted to be chased. In the schoolyard, they ran and laughed and played along with the boys. I guess you could say we were playing "grab-ass."

There was a Science teacher who had several animals in his classroom and he would let students come play with them before school. His classroom was located outside of the main building in a trailer. He would allow us to take the snakes and hamsters outside the cages. We students would go and pick up the snakes and take them around the playground prior to school.

In the third grade, Rayshon, Ned, Andre, and I performed a song in front of our class. I saw it as an easy way to get the attention of the class on us. Our teacher, Senora Hernandez, allowed us to perform in front of the other students upon our request. Our song had a rhythm, dance moves, and a melody to go along with it. Each person had a special part and contribution in the performance. The melody went as like, "Doodoo do Doodoo do Doodoo do Doodoo do." After that, we all started to snap our fingers and dance in concert. I don't remember the whole song, but some of the lyrics were, "You think you're all cool, you ain't nothing but a fool, you think you're all bad, you ain't nothing but a crab." The original lyrics said fag, but we had to make sure it was appropriate for the classroom. I remember Andreas would slide forward on his knees when his part came and point towards his underwear. When we finished performing, the class and Senora Hernandez applauded and was pleased. We gained a lot of popularity from our little publicity stunt.

During elementary school, we also had the DARE program in the public education school system. Dare stood for Drug Abuse Resistance Education and was aimed at keeping kids off drugs and away from crime. DARE, actually introduced me to some drugs I was not aware of as well. That was the first time I had ever seen crack or heroin in an image. As a kid, it all looked like poison to me. Our assigned officer for the school was named Officer Mitchell. He was a bald head, light-skinned man with a thick mustache. He was very relatable and educated me on the dangers that were present beyond the classroom. I took the information he shared seriously and I learned from it what I could. In fact, I was selected as one of the finalists for the DARE essay contest that year. I still remember the beginning of my essay saying "I choose to be drug-free and violence-free because I know the harmful effects that drugs can have on my friends, family, and people in my community." Winning the essay contest was important to me and it made me feel good about myself. This may have been the first major individual accomplishment in my lifetime.

The following year, the Foreign Language program was discontinued at Mt. Airy and continued at Heinold Foreign Language Academy. The school was located on the west side of town and I was not thrilled about relocating schools, but my opinion of the move quickly changed. I was relieved as most of my friends from Mt. Airy had made the transition to Heinold as well. Not only did they offer the Spanish program at Heinold, but they also offered a French program, too. I loved attending the school, and the challenges I faced academically and socially. All subjects, other than English class, were taught in Spanish. I learned Math, Science, and Social Studies all in Spanish. I would have to translate the words before I could complete the work. I made friends in the French and Spanish programs at various grade levels in the school.

There were two security guards at the school who were both positive male role models for me growing. Their names were Mr. Shipman and Mr. Walker. These men looked tough and intimidating, but they were steadfast and showed caring in their interactions with students. They showed us tough love, but

I always felt safe in school with them patrolling the campus. Mr. Walker was excellent about placing himself in hot spot areas during transition times. I could not get away with anything without them knowing about it. As soon as I thought no one was looking, Mr. Walker would mysteriously come from around the corner. He would redirect me by always questioning, "Where are you going, Eric?" If I didn't know, he would grab me by the rim of my shirt and escort me there. Mr. Shipman and Mr. Walker were both well-liked and respected by all the students

I also remember drawing the school logo for Heinold. There was an art competition for the design and my drawing was selected. The drawing depicted the letters that spelled out Heinold, with a globe substituted for the O. The school mascot, an eagle, was perched above the O as well. I received recognition and was happy to see the image on items such as t-shirts and mugs. However, my mother held the position that I should have been paid for the image. Looking back, she was absolutely right about me deserving some form of compensation for my artwork. As a kid, I was content with receiving clout from my classmates and within the school.

I was militant as a student and had a burning desire to know my African-American history and ancestry. I wondered where I had come from and who my ancestors were. The world I lived in emphasized to me that I was bound to be a rapper or an athlete, but my intellect would not accept this illusion of reality. My fifth-grade year was a defining time in my childhood. I probably had earned the reputation amongst teachers and staff as a smart student, who went against the rules. I became more disobedient as a student and questioned the status quo in the curriculum. Each year, white American history was reinforced in an effort to assimilate students to the culture within this country. I had grown tired of this narrative and challenged it within many of my classrooms. To some teachers, certainly,

my outspokenness may have just seemed like a behavioral issue. However, my rebellion against the curriculum was rooted
in black pride and a blessed assurance. I knew the world was
much bigger and there was more to learn than what was being
shown to me from the textbook.

One time, my fearless nature naturally had an opportunity
to encounter authority. As I stated, all of the classes at Heinold
were taught in foreign languages, so the same was for my
Social Studies class. The teacher, a different Senora Hernandez, seemed uninterested in the lessons she was teaching us. I
had grown tired of learning the same old stuff in class. It was
much of the same American history we had been assimilated
with years prior. I observed how the students were not engaged
in Senora Hernandez's lesson. We were bored and she was simply filing papers and being authoritative from the desk. I raised
my hand to ask a question and she eventually acknowledged
me, with a scowl on her face. I examined, *"Senora Hernandez,
Porque no estudiamos la historia de Africano Americanos?"* In
English, I asked her why we weren't studying African American history. She swiftly replied in English with, "Excuse me?"
I then responded back in English with, *"Senora Hernandez, we
have a classroom full of black students, so why aren't we learning any black history?"* The classroom gasped from my bold
and reproachful question. The teacher coldly declared, "Because it's not in the curriculum, so I don't have to teach it!" Of
course, this answer to my question did not satisfy my thirst for
knowledge about my history. Senora Hernandez had seen my
line of questioning as contempt and shortly after the incident,
she sent me to Mrs. Willis's class.

Mrs. Onva Willis was my English teacher, but at this time
she must have been the team leader. I was not sent to the office, but rather to her classroom to receive discipline for my
insolence. At that time, I had never really bonded with any of
the teachers at Heinold. Mrs. Willis was only the second black

teacher I ever had, since kindergarten with Miss Berry. Mrs. Willis was a strong and intelligent woman, who demanded respect and she got it from all students. Before this point, I simply thought of Mrs. Willis as a strict English teacher.

On this particular day, Mrs. Willis and I discussed the incident that had occurred in the Social Studies classroom with Mrs. Hernandez. Without judgment, she listened to my story and quickly realized that my defiance was really a cry out for freedom. After actively listening, this wise teacher told me three words that I will never forget. She kindly approached me with a smile and insisted, "Use your resources!" At first, I did not understand what she meant. I continued to gaze at her as I tried to decode what she had just instructed me to do. She confidently looked at me as if she could see me thinking about a resolution. I then asked her, "*What do you mean?*" She responded, "You can read can't you?" I responded quickly affirming, "*Yes.*" Mrs. Willis countered with, "There is nothing stopping you from going into the library and reading about your people if that is what you want to do." At that moment, I finally realized what those three words meant. I realized that I had been misplacing my anger towards Mrs. Hernandez and needed to channel that energy and passion towards my own discovery. I took her advice and in my opinion, it liberated me academically. I started to take ownership of my learning and sought out to do research about as much African history as I could find.

Internally, I knew that there was much more for me than being a rapper or athlete, as society suggested. I didn't know what it was, but I knew that God had created me for a greater purpose. I was energized and enthused learning about people like Benjamin Banneker, George Washington Carver, Elijah McCoy, Garrett Morgan, and Jan Ernst Matzeliger. Men like Frederick Douglass, Malcolm X, and Booker T became key historical idols and representations of what I could become. Booker T.

Washington helped me discover and define my own identity within my race. I was encouraged to find out that Frederick Douglas was known for being a dynamic orator. With my talkativeness, I was able to make a connection to the fact that he was most famous for public speaking. At that time, I was getting in trouble for speaking out in the classroom. I received confirmation through Douglas that my voice could be used for the good of society and to help others. Malcolm X taught me to be bold in my pursuit of freedom and to use my intelligence against all odds.

Mrs. Willis did not stop there, and has become a person I can truly consider my hero! She steered me away from being a disrespectful student and challenged me to reach my fullest potential. She prevented me from being labeled as a troubled kid and helped redirect my energy positively towards knowledge and education. She empowered me as a student by sharing her wisdom, expecting self-efficacy, and giving me valuable guidance. I applied the strategy she gave me throughout my childhood and it made a massive impact on my life. It allowed me to not be so resistant, but rather learn as much as I could from the American and African history I was exposed to. Mrs. Willis did more for me than she probably knows. I was amazed at how she used her platform as a teacher to transform my life and the lives of many others. I developed as my passion for learning my history ignited and fueled changes in my early life. From that point forward, any reports or assignments that Mrs. Willis assigned were predominately about African American content and culture. She would still rigorously teach the curriculum when it was necessary, but the students didn't resist her because she had already built trusting relationships.

Mrs. Willis, with her responsive teaching strategies, started infusing the type of lessons many of us students desired within the curriculum. I had no idea that black people had a National Anthem prior to her class. We studied *Lift Every Voice* as a literary piece and then she taught us to sing the song as a classroom. She got the help of Mr. Shipman, the security guard, to arrange us vocally. He must have been a deacon or something with experience in the church choir. He arranged us in groups of sopranos, altos, and tenors. He organized us and they both taught our classroom how to sing the anthem. We put all of our hearts into it and sang every word with fury and conviction. We were even asked to sing the song at a performance that year for our parents, other students, and the community. We connected with the words from an authentic place of identification. The intrinsic value of the song was worth much more than what could be heard by the ear.

Heinold was also the place where I had my first major fight in middle school. It was with a classmate named Rayshon, who was actually my friend for many years. It all happened because of some playful name-calling, which turned personal. I remember it like it was yesterday. We were in gym class, which was located on the lower floor of the school building. In the front left corner of the gym, there was a large cooling fan that was blowing because there was no air condition. Several of the students were hanging out near the fan and that is where the whole incident occurred.

This was the day that Ray and I decided to go and say silly things into the fan - the fan blowing, our voices would transform into a robotic or alien type of sound. Many of the students found this act to be entertaining. At first, it was all fun and games as Rayshon and I exchanged phrases and comments. When we ran out of things to say, we started to launch insults towards each other. The verbal barbs were about personal things that we knew about each other. I called him an egghead or something like that and then he got me mad when he responded with, "Bitch, ass, momma!" He recently had a dog that passed away, so I returned fire by saying in the fan, *"Dead, ass, dog!"* The kids who were witnessing the confrontation were antagonizing, laughing, and instigating the whole time. My comment must have struck a nerve because Rayshon marched to the fan and said, "Handi, cap, brother!" I went from zero to ten and immediately punched Rayshon in the face as he turned and walked away from the fan. I remember the momentum from the punch causing him to fly through the gym's double doors, which led upstairs to the main floor.

After he got up, I back-pedaled myself into a win in my first junior high fight. I already had landed a solid strike, so I moved backward while dodging and keeping my guard up to defend his attacks. I avoided his charge like a matador does a bull and nullified any possible counter-attack from Rayshon. I threw a few more punches to keep him back, but the fight was broken up shortly after. In my mind, I had already proved my point but truly didn't want to be fighting with my friend. I guess you can say we were caught up in the emotions of the situation more than anything. It was a prime example of playing that led to fighting. Both of our comments were inappropriate and two wrongs don't make a right. I was rightfully sent to In-School Suspension or ISS for three days for my infraction. I thought my Mother would be proud of me for defending her. Instead, she was upset about me getting into trouble. She emphasized, "He doesn't know me; who cares what he calls me?" After that, I felt silly for allowing my emotions to get the better of me with a close friend.

I do remember getting in trouble once for putting a worm in the Art teacher's chair on April Fool's day. I must have been planning the prank since I had the worm with me in the classroom. The teacher stepped out of the classroom for a short period of time and I made my move. The biggest mistake I made was announcing the deed to my classmates. The teacher returned, and we all waited with anticipation for Ms. Kat to squash the worm on her pants. However, Ms. Kat had looked down prior to sitting in the seat. She picked the worm up with a pencil and asked, "Who put this worm in my seat?" Every kid in the classroom pointed to me and I was busted. I learned then and there to keep my pranks to myself and simply enjoy the reactions anonymously.

I was sent to the principal for the prank, where I met the dreaded Senora Fontana. She was a small, petite, elder Hispanic woman. She walked with a hunch in her back and was notorious for carrying a large mug of coffee around. I sat down in a chair in the middle of her office and she was about tired of seeing me misbehave. She grilled me and threatened me with the options she had for consequences to my actions. She spoke directly in front of my face, which introduced me to her dragon breath from drinking coffee. Sitting in her office and smelling her breath was cruel and unusual punishment. I was eventually given a consequence and was sent back to class. I returned after absorbing the wrath of the coffee breath with a frown on my face. Chris, who got in trouble often, was laughing hysterically and it was making me further upset. I tried to ignore him, but he continued to try to get my attention. I finally acknowledged him and asked him what he wanted. In laughter he questioned, "You mad, she breathed on you didn't she!" I had no choice, but to laugh off the traumatic experience.

Another memorable time at Heinold was when I participated in a Motown tribute and performed ABC by the Jackson Five with some of my classmates. It was Jermaine, but I coordinated the costumes and dance steps into a magnificent performance. I was in charge of the choreography and dance routine, but we all collaborated on the song. The teacher allowed us to practice in the hallway during class time. I had possession of an old guitar at the time and had access to wardrobe items by rummaging through my sister's items. It started as a project for Social Studies, but eventually, it evolved into musical performances and a show. In fact, after performing it for the school, the principal asked us to perform the song at the upcoming spring carnival as well. It was a big hit amongst the school body!

The members of the group were Rayshon (Jackie), Dion (Michael), Will (Marlon), Jacob (Tito), and I (Jermaine). Jacob was actually a white kid who went to school with us for several years. We tried to make sure everybody had a part in the song where they were highlighted. We had even enlisted the help of some girls in the class as groupies. Their job was to run to the stage with excitement and get the crowd involved and excited when we came out. We did not tell the girls they were groupies. I believe we referred to them as cheerleaders. It was hilarious and awesome at the same time! They made tons of noise when we came out, which was awesome and a major addition to the performance. They were just as much a part of the show as we were. Dion was a friend of mine, who had a swagger of his own. He was a Michael Jackson and music fan, so he knew the lyrics to the song and was a natural performer. He had the energy, charisma, and flair for the lead singer position.

There was plenty of air grinding and pelvic thrusts through-out the musical showcase. By the time the Spring Carnival came, the original Jackson 5 members were starting to break up like most groups. I can't remember exactly what he was up-set about, but losing Dion right before the spring performance was a big deal. It was a major loss to the show and we were scrambling to fill the role. Then came Darius; He was a grade above us, but was more than willing to fill in and save the group for the performance. Darius had a carelessness about himself that sold the show and made it still entertaining. He had his own interpretation of the main Michael Jackson part, which was enough for us to get by. However, Dion was the real Mike.

The last major event that happened at Heinold was when I got expelled from the school. During that time, we commonly played war in the neighborhood with fake guns. I had a Nautica jacket that had many pockets on it that I would wear while we played. The number of pockets made it easy to carry several items. We would gather all the neighborhood boys and fake guns we could muster and run around in a cops and robbers type of war game. When we played, nobody ever wanted to die of course or be caught empty-handed, so I packed my pockets full of fake weapons.

The following day, I wore the same Nautica jacket to school. I didn't intentionally take the fake gun to school, but I did realize it was in my pocket shortly after I left home. It was a broken cap gun with the barrel removed and an orange tip on it. It was wrapped in masking tape, which I had colored black with a marker. I could have taken it back, but I was more concerned about not missing the bus. My plan was to not make a big deal about it and make it through my school day without anyone noticing. At the end of the school day, as I was transitioning from one class to another, I was running a little bit late. I threw my jacket over my shoulder in a mad rush to get to class on time. When I slung my jacket, the cap gun fell out of my pocket and on the floor right in front of the science teacher Mrs. Lawler. I remember her picking it up with one finger as if it was a real munition. It was obviously fake, but she handled it like it was a nuclear weapon. I knew I was in trouble from the moment the cap gun fell on the ground.

Soon after the occurrence, I was called to the office where I met the principal. She had no other choice but to expel me. This meant I would be suspended from school for the rest of the year. Rather than wait for the result, my mother decided to remove me from that school and put me into a new school district. Luckily for me, this happened much before kids started bringing guns to school and contributing to mass shootings. The issue was still handled very seriously and processed as such, but I know my consequences could have been much worse. Afterward, I went to Finneytown Middle School for the remainder of the seventh and eighth grades.

Finneytown was a great school during the time I attended there and challenged me academically. This was the first school I had been to that was not a foreign language academy. The majority of the students were white, but there were enough black people for me to find some friends. One of those friends was named Dee. Dee was hilarious and a well-known comedian and class clown. It was hard not to laugh at the jokes he told. I remember being reprimanded or re-directed several times for laughing uncontrollably in response to Dee's antics. In fact, he and I performed Michael Jackson's Thriller for a school talent show my first year there. He wore a grim reaper mask with a suit and I wore a Thriller jacket my sister had with a vampire mask. It was a great performance and was applauded by the student body. We didn't win, but the performance made me popular among social circles going forward. People were curious who the guy dancing with Dee was.

There was also a kid in my class named Adam. He was a bit weird socially, but he had a great sense of humor and was extremely smart. He knew how to travel anywhere in the country and could tell you the exact highways to get there. Adam was hilarious, and when he would laugh he would empathetically bang on the desk with his hand. Our math teacher would have his hands full trying to contain Adam and me when Dee was on a roll. I tried hard to stay cool, calm and collected in the classroom. However, once Dee started to act up and Adam started joyously laughing out loud and banging his hand, I could control myself no longer. I felt compelled to join in on the fun.

Another friend I had was Tyler. He was quiet and reserved, but we would hang out and play sports together after school some days. We both decided to try out for the middle school basketball team our eighth-grade year. I made the A team, but Tyler was sent to the developmental team B. In friendship, I voided my opportunity with the A team to play with him on the B team. We had fun that year and enjoyed playing alongside one another as teammates. I also made the baseball team that year and played for the team as well. I had another friend named Joe, with who I sometimes would play video games and street hockey. He loved hockey and I loved to skate, so I did my best to pick up the pastime. Joe and Tyler were both nice towards me and the friendships made me feel more comfortable at the new school.

Finneytown was a culture shock for me academically and socially, but I appreciated the experience. I was able to find my own lane, but it was definitely a predominantly white school. In eighth grade, I took and passed the Walnut Hills test. It was timely because my brother and I were reported to the school district for living outside of the community limits. My mother and Creester were separating at this time. Come to find out, Creester had gone to the district and told them we were using a false address to attend the school. In fact, my mother did use one of her customer addresses in order for us to register in the school. My brother and I were removed from the school district by the end of that year. It really didn't matter at that point because my mother was raving about me passing the test and going to Walnut Hills. I wasn't sure what that meant at the time, but little did I know it was my gateway to success.

I attended Walnut Hills High School for ninth through twelfth grade. Walnut is a prestigious school nationally, which is located in Cincinnati, Ohio. My mother was adamant about me doing well at the school during my high school years. She would often say, "I didn't go up there and show them people you was smart, *you did*!" That was her way of asserting that I had no excuse for not doing well in the magnet school. The expectations were high for me upon entering Walnut Hills for my high school years.

It took some adjusting, but I was eventually able to maintain decent grades in my first year. I remember learning how to type during my ninth grade year and how to catch the city's

Metro bus system. I continued Spanish at Walnut, taking the highest level I could as a ninth-grader to fulfill my foreign language requirements. I needed two years of a foreign language for graduation, so I took the level below the highest level to make sure I could exclusively in Spanish. I became acclimated to the enhanced learning environment and set my sights on a path of exploration.

There were several people I knew who attended the school with me. Some students were prior classmates, prior teammates, and some people I just knew from around the city. I also found out that I had a cousin who attended the school. My Mother had started to talk to me about a boy, who was her half-sister's son. I did not know Aunt Nat was my actual aunt until high school. My Mom told me his name was Neico, but little did she know, Neico and I had already connected. We had become familiar with one another due to having mutual friends and social groups. We grew even closer once we knew that we shared the same blood. Neico and I were as thick as thieves during high school. There was a mutual bond that connected us as friends. We all wanted to go to college and we all were looking to have fun on the journey.

I made friends at the school easily and quickly developed a crew of people I hung around. The crew was composed of mutual friends between Neico and I. Ned has been my friend since kindergarten, but we were separated during middle school. When the Spanish program discontinued at Mt. Airy, Ned's parents sent him to Roselawn Condon, where he met Neico. Ned was always our voice of reason within the group. Whenever we took things too far, Ned would always warn us by saying, "Maaaaaan." Once he said that we would all redirect our energy with some awareness of the consequences.

Tony was another person in our squad. Neico knew Tony from before, but we didn't become friends until Walnut. Tony was the best dancer in our crew and our secret weapon during dance battles at parties. He had mastered the airwalk and was an excellent performer in the clutch. Tony was confident, strong, and hilarious to be around growing up. His mother passed away during our time in high school, and I was always impressed by his ability to persevere through the hardship.

White Mike, was a white kid who grew up the same way we did in Cincinnati. He was a great rapper and was very culturally aware, so he was able to relate to us seamlessly. He probably knew more about rap and black people than we did at the time. We had to call him White Mike to remind ourselves that he was white because his behavior and mentality was definitely black. He was a loyal friend, who was assigned to talking to the police whenever we got in trouble. For some reason, the cops would always pull him aside to ask what was going on anyway. Talking to the cops was his job and assignment on the nights we went out and he played a vital role as well.

Denzel was a new kid from Florida, who started at Walnut in the ninth grade. He was friends with Mike, so we happily accepted him into our group. Denzel was smart, charming with the ladies, and fun to be around. He was a fish out of water relocating from Florida to Cincinnati. He was shy at first and I could tell he was a bit sheltered growing up. Nonetheless, he still was interested in having a good time, so he meshed well with the rest of us. He quickly learned our social norms and provided our group with an additional place to hang out. We had plenty of fun at his apartment during high school. Denzel and Mike are how John became associated with us. John came from an affluent upbringing, but he did his best to keep up with us as well

Matthew lived in my neighborhood and we became cool due to riding the same bus. I remember him wearing a sky blue and black Kango hat during the first week of school. They likely belonged to his dad, but Matthew wore them as a way to express who he saw himself to be. Matthew was a budding rap star too and we would often exchange flows on the bus after school. We would pass notes during biology class, exchanging rap bars with one another. His parents were always nice to me, so they would let me come over to their house and visit. He was a good friend most of the time, but I learned that he had some shady ways about him. He was close to me, so I would tell him secrets about my encounters with girls. I found out later that he was going behind my back and giving full reports back to the girls to earn favor. He did this a couple of times before I caught on. I still accepted him for who he was, but I kept him out of my personal business moving forward.

Chauncey and I became friends out of circumstance, but he had made friends with Neico previously. Chauncey was in my history class and was just funny within his own right. He had charisma and was an extremely outgoing and social person. In class one day, he informed me about him being chased home in the neighborhood by a kid with a machete. He was concerned about walking home because of the threat, so I volunteered to drive him there. He was relieved and appreciated the protection he was afforded. We became close friends after that car ride home. In fact, I would often pick Chauncey up before school once he moved closer to my house. I didn't mind because it was on my way to school and I enjoyed his company. Chauncey sometimes had access to cigars and weed, so he played the role of the risk-taking and experimental member in our group.

John was actually an important member of the crew because of his connections. His father owned a radio station in the city and John was the editor for the school newspaper. This came in handy when my crew had a conflict with another crew over a rap battle. The opposing crew had made a crap album under the alias "Wolfpack." My crew and I were not impressed with the release and decided to make a diss song in response. I already had a problem with one of the members of the Wolfpack, so the diss song just heightened the tension. We named our song "Wolfcrap." This was my first time recording, but the song turned out fairly well. It became popular amongst my peers and started a bit of controversy within the school. However, John wrote a favorable article in the school newspaper for our crew. It highlighted our song and gave an impression of victory towards the rap battle. John was also tied in with the white social groups, so once he became a part of our crew we were invited to all of the "white parties." Those parties always included heavier drug use, but my friends and I simply went to have a good time.

That is how I met Pounds. Pounds was a cool and caring white girl, who loved to hang around my crew. She was a pretty girl, but I was not interested in her being my girlfriend. I'm sure she liked me at that time, but I was too involved in my life to pay her close enough attention. Either way, I always considered Pounds as a good friend. She would always communicate to me where the white parties were going to be. In fact, when my car broke down, Pounds would come and pick me up for school, so I didn't have to catch the bus. I appreciated her friendship, especially during my latter high school years.

Although Walnut was a high school, it also included a junior high for seventh and eighth-graders. I learned that seventh graders were nicknamed, "Effies." Due to taking Latin in seventh grade, several students would get F's and flunk out of the school. The eighth-graders were called "E-flats." I am sure there was some derogatory reason why eighth-graders were referred to by that name. Whether an Effie or an E-flat, you had to be on guard from hazing and upperclassmen pranks. The junior high kids were constant targets due to being the low fish on the totem pole. Before school, all of the students would report to the cafeteria until all of the buses arrived and class began. There were some mats in the cafeteria, so any junior high student who came in the cafeteria was subject to a body slam, power bombs, or suplex on the gym mats. Other times, an Effie might be seen being dragged by their backpacks down the hallway. It sounds much crueler than it was, but the lower classmen participated and it was only done in good fun.

I was quite the prankster in high school, but I had learned from my past blunders how to get away without anyone knowing. I learned how to order things off the internet, and soon after purchased some stink bombs that reeked horribly. One vile could stink up an entire hallway. The stink bomb was in a thin glass container, so the smell would be dispersed once the glass cracked. I would wait until right before the bell rang in a well-traveled hallway. Once the bell rang, I would throw the vile and wait to hear it crack. The sound was like, "Tink, tink, tink, tink, tink, crunch!" Upon hearing the crunch, I braced myself for the chaos and comedy that would ensue. You could hear the students complaining about the smell and see others running down the hallway to escape the potent aroma. I posted up on a locker and laughed hysterically as it looked like people were scrambling for their lives.

I would also do things like play car wars. While driving, I would throw items out the window at cars my friends were commuting. If the car was behind me, I would launch things like lotion or a bottle of bubbles. I'm not sure why I had the bubbles, but one time, I was able to detonate the bubbles on the hood of a friend's car. I had no idea of the damage it could cause, but it actually stained the hood of my friend's car. Afterward, she told me later that she got in trouble with her father for the car hood and we laughed about it together. I now realize this was extremely dangerous, but as a teen, I was solely concerned with having a good time.

As I became more popular in the following years, it was much more difficult to keep up with my academics. This was especially true when the high school girls came into the picture. I had a car by tenth grade, so my access to girls and partying was expanded. I started to smoke socially with my friends after school and on the weekends. We would smoke mini cigars to and from school, but we experimented with pot at parties and socially. Due to the way I lost my Dad, I never had a desire to experiment with anything beyond weed. To me, the high from marijuana was as high as I was trying to go. I remember having a few drinks socially, but I didn't have a real drink of alcohol until shortly after high school.

I had an epic time in high school, but my partying and popularity negatively affected my grades. I did my best to keep my bad report cards away from my Mother, but she often asked for mine once my brothers received theirs - I am guilty of even having a friend of mine change my grades on the computer. I was busted by my mother one time when I desperately changed an F to a B with a pencil. My Mother easily detected my deception, and my faking of my grades, of course, became shop news for a period of time. It was definitely an embarrassing moment in my life. I tried to run away from the truth, but the truth was much faster.

By junior year, I was playing varsity football and my popularity was at an all-time high. I was caught up in who I was socially and began to lose sight of the opportunity I had at Walnut Hills. My ego met its match when I encountered Ms. Chow. She was an ancient Chinese lady who taught Chemistry at Walnut and was known for failing several students each year. She spoke broken English and I underestimated her from the moment enter her classroom, but Ms. Chow taught me a very valuable lesson in making choices.

Ms. Chow had an odd personality and immediately she rubbed me the wrong way. I could not understand most of what she was saying, nor did I relate to her sense of humor. She would attempt to call students out in class and this did not sit with me well. Ms. Chow had a large jar of jelly beans and would pass them out to all of the good students. I rarely received a jelly bean from her. She would smile as she passed out the jelly bean to the person sitting in front of me. As soon as she turned towards me, she would lower her eyes and give a blank facial expression. Ms. Chow would often pronounce, "Isaacs, no jelly bean for you." I felt demotivated by the approach, so I started telling jokes and focused on having a good time during class. I would win the battles, but Ms. Chow was focused on winning the war.

She informed each student from the beginning, "If you miss two of my assignments, you fail!" I did not take her seriously and had to learn my lesson the hard way. After missing a couple of assignments, Ms. Chow told me the only way we could pass was to come to her help night for an hour and a half on Wednesdays. Ignorantly, I did not attend the help nights and failed the chemistry class my junior year. My friend Ned wisely heeded the advice and sacrificed his Wednesday evenings. No wonder he was able to pass the class and I was forced to make up the credits in summer school. Due to my constant clowning in the class, every student who sat around me in class accompanied me in summer school. I learned that you can either lead people the right way or you can lead folks the wrong way. I also learned about the harsh consequences of my actions. As a result of failing chemistry, I was academically ineligible to play football my senior season. It was a major disappointment to myself and my teams. If I could do it over again, I would have stayed for those help nights and did my best to pass the class. However, sometimes in life you only get one chance to do things the right way.

Due to failing the class, the school threatened to kick me out for the upcoming senior year. A meeting was scheduled between the Principal, my Mom, and I. During the exit meeting, I was able to convince the principal to give me another opportunity to remain in the school. I took full responsibility for my academic performance and apologized to him and my mother.

I also guaranteed Mr. K that given another chance, I would not get less than a 'C' all year. He was moved by my gift of gab and gave me another opportunity. Fortunately, I didn't have to move schools for my senior year. I maintained a 3.2-grade point average from that time moving forward. It proved to me that I could have sustained a high-grade point average for all four years. It was all a matter of whether or not I applied myself.

I didn't realize it while in school, but I have always been a natural-born leader amongst my peers. At Golden Skates, I was the first one in my crew to jump 'on' something each holiday event. I was the first one comfortable with the opposite sex, so my friends learned how to talk to and approach girls. In fact, many of my friends only had access to certain girls through an association with me. I was active in the streets, so some of my friends were only welcomed at certain parties when they were with me. My friends learned from me how to carry themselves around girls and in dangerous situations. The code I used to indicate to my friends to be on their best behavior was, "Violations are on!" With violations on, anybody who violated the acceptable behavior at that moment was punched and ridiculed. I was the first to have a car and the first to have sex. I was also the first to introduce pot into the equation. I was the first one of us to possess it and the first to learn how to roll a blunt, which I learned from observing family members. Although I was the leader of my crew, I didn't recognize the leadership qualities until much later in life.

Walnut Hills was an outstanding school and it allowed me to fully expand my wings. The school was rich in culture and diversity. The classes and curriculum challenged me to my greatest potential. My mind was stretched and developed during those formidable years. Without a doubt, Walnut Hills prepared me intellectually for the world I would face and was a phenomenal educational and social experience. I always dreamed that one of my children would follow my lead and attend the school as well. The standards of the institutions and the rigorous instruction are second to none. I dreamt about one day my future kids attending and graduating from Walnut as well. I am thankful and grateful for being allowed to benefit from the rigorous institutions of education I attended. God used education to inform and prepare me for life. He showed me the full power of my brain and the intelligence he gifted me with. However, the majority of the lessons I learned were not in the textbook, but rather outside the classroom.

The fear of the Lord is the beginning of knowledge; fools despise wisdom and instruction." **Proverbs 1:7**

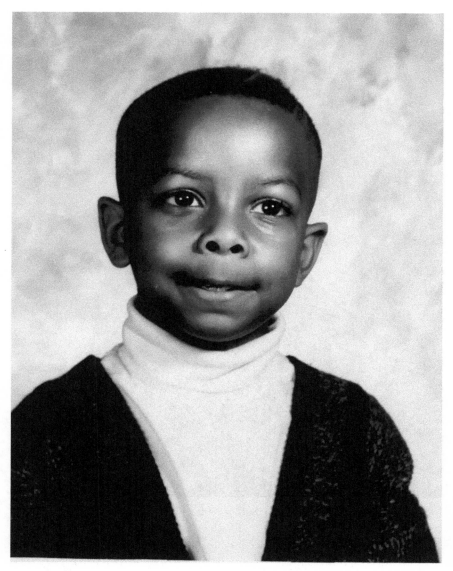

Kindergarten

Senior Year

Chapter 12

Fish for a Lifetime

"For even when we were with you, this we commanded you, that if any would not work, neither should he eat." **2nd Thessalonians 3:10**

I have always understood the concept of money, but it has never been very important to me. I consider my efforts at the age of eight or nine to make pocket change at my Mother's salon as my first job. I remember selling lemonade outside the beauty salon. Some of the ladies would support my efforts and I would get enough money to go to the corner store and buy snacks. I often would try to sell people drawings or find other creative ways to earn cash. When I was young, I received money from doing chores for my Grandma Sarah around the beauty salon; this included washing the windows and taking out the trash.

Before that, I had made money by carrying groceries for elderly people in my neighborhood. While out riding my bike, I would look for people returning home from the grocery store and offer help. Sometimes, I would end up being paid the change they had in their pockets. Other times, I would leave with an apple. Either way, any reward for my labor was appreciated. It was a wonderful feeling to bring in my own money for the work I provided, but the bounty was inconsequential.

When I was 13, I was old enough to pursue my first official job. There was a program in Cincinnati, Ohio, called CCY. The organization helped kids in the city stay off the streets by offering them part-time summer employment. I started the job hunt late that summer, so by the time I was registered, there were only a few jobs available. I was employed by CCY and I quickly learned the value and true meaning of hard work.

I was employed as a janitor at a nearby high school, Aiken, where my sister Tera went to school and graduated from. I was familiar with the facility but clueless about the lessons I would learn from the experience. My working tools consisted of a freeze can, a putty knife, and a mop bucket. I was taught how to mop in a figure-eight pattern and how to manage my time and energy effectively. I spent that summer cleaning up restrooms and scraping gum off of the bottom of chairs and desks. If I ever got bored, I would look for an insect to freeze. I grew newfound respect for janitors and their toil. I also figured out that janitorial work was not the career path I wanted to pursue in the future. I vividly remember the feeling of riding my bike home from work with a check in my pocket. It was only $125, but it made me feel like a young man.

Working was a positive experience for me, so I made sure to be on time with my registration the following year. Due to my attending a Foreign Language Academy, I was employed at a place called the Smart Lab during my second year. Working for CCY taught me how to use the public transportation system because I caught the metro bus downtown and walked a few blocks to get to the job.

At the Smart Lab, I was joined by about fifteen other kids and three mentors. We learned different things like digital design, flight simulators, video production, and other structural types of projects. I was influenced by rap culture, so I would often create compact disc covers during my exploration time. At that time, I believed my first rap album would be called "Big Things Come in Small Packages." I would make graphic designs for album covers for other friends who had rap dreams as well. I spent a lot of time on the flight simulators, computers, and video recording equipment, too. I recorded interviews and learned the basic techniques and principles of video recording. I was being paid for furthering my knowledge and continuing to learn during the summer. It was an awesome summer job experience and it piqued my curiosity in several different areas.

A moment of fame came that summer when the students were asked to participate in a bridge-building competition. The objective was to build a bridge using nothing but toothpicks and school glue. I did some research on bridge designs and noticed how triangles and squares were used in many of their structural designs. I used those same concepts in the design of my bridge. After some work time, each bridge was put to the test in a pressure machine. My bridge happened to hold 110 pounds and won the competition! The Smart Lab was so impressed that a newspaper article was written and I was later interviewed by a reporter. My mother still has this article to this day. It was a time in my life when I realized I could do anything if I put my mind to it. I started to stretch my understanding and desire for learning new things.

"I can do all things through Christ who strengthens me."
Philippians 4:13

The next summer, the CCY program was shut down for some political reasons beyond my control or imagination. I had a desire to continue working because I was fifteen and I knew driving was something I wanted to do in the near future. I needed money for driving school and a car, so I applied for a bagger position at a local grocery called K Roger's. I called two days after turning in an application, to express my interest in the position. I received a callback, interviewed for the position, and was able to secure the job fairly easily. It was a pretty cool job and I liked the fast-paced nature.

My buddy Shane had already been working for K Rogers by the time I arrived. However, Shane had actually gone into business for himself on the side. He would steal cartons of Newport cigarettes from the store and sell them to the neighborhood ice cream truck for $15 each. The company eventually caught onto his scheme and Shane was terminated a few months after I started. Once he left the job, it wasn't as fun to work there, but I stayed for another year or so. His brother, Delvin, and I still made the most of our time working there.

My duties included bagging up groceries for customers, gathering carts from the parking lot, and cleaning up the occasional mess. Baggers were also responsible for cleaning the restrooms, but lucky enough I never was asked to perform that task. I mastered the art of bagging quickly and efficiently. I grew a fan base of customers who frequented my lines to enjoy my services. Sometimes, customers would ask me for assistance with their groceries to the car. I would agree and once outside, the customer would offer me a tip. We were not supposed to accept tips from customers, but many of them would insist that I took the tip. It would have done more damage to the company by offending the customer, so I would accept the given change in the spirit of not being rude. I remember an older sophisticated white woman, who preferred for me to handle her groceries. I learned that people find comfort in a simple smile and peace of mind in knowing their groceries were packed in order. I learned from and relished the socialization at the grocery store. I became pretty fast and efficient with bagging and professional with my customer service.

After mastering the art of bagging groceries, I set my sights and attention on the cash register. I was intrigued by the cashiers, and a bit envious that the cashiers made a little more money than the baggers. Cashiers not only made more money but weren't forced to deal with the elements outside when retrieving carts. Rain, sleet, or snow, the manager would call over the intercom saying, "Eric carts please." Sometimes it was okay for the fresh air, but other times I just simply didn't feel like going out in the weather. I still found a way to embrace the freedom and independence from being outside. It was time that I felt like I wasn't being supervised while performing my job.

I don't remember ever being asked to fully clean the bathrooms, but I remember a few major accidents that I was forced to clean up. One time, in particular, I wasn't very happy about it. A lady came in the store with her child strapped to her back in some sort of backpack-style child carrier. She came into the store and immediately headed for the aisle that she needed to visit. Before she could make it down the aisle, her child had begun to poop in the child carrier. Once it overloaded the seat, the poop started to drip and leave a trail. It was all over the poor lady's back and several of the employees saw the accident unfold. Some of the front end employees and I were reacting dramatically and laughing about what we witnessed. All of a sudden, Chris came over the intercom and said, "Eric, clean up aisle nine." I was in disbelief and it was at that moment I realized my days as a bagger were numbered. I grumbled and complained all the way through the task, while my co-workers laughed at my dismay. I believed in an honest day's work, but this was one of those times where it would have been nice to have already been on carts. This was a lesson in learning that poop rolls downhill. I had God-given abilities and skills that I had not fully applied yet.

I quickly learned as much about the registers as possible. I observed and picked the brains of cashiers who were willing to share the information with me. I never received any formal training, but I was able to gain the knowledge required for cashiering and handling a register. One day, we were extremely busy and down a few cashiers. I told the manager that I could cashier and to give me a shot. The manager Chris was reluctant, but amidst the growing line and customer complaints, the manager decided he had no other alternative. I was nervous as he walked towards me with the register and put me on the express lane closest to him. I soon got the hang of it and became comfortable with the process. The manager was impressed and thankful for me saving the day. From that point on, my cart runs were minimal and the manager knew he had an additional cashier when needed. Whenever we started to get busy, I would look over and he would wave his hand for me to come and get a register. At least, if I was on the register, that was time away from hearing, "Eric, carts please." No!

I saved up my money and was able to pay for my driving school. The fee was $425. The school did a good job teaching me the rules of driving and giving me experience behind the wheel. I passed the written and driving tests on the first attempts and my mother found me a car for $1600. My first vehicle was bought at a yard sale and was a 1991 Hyundai Scoupe. It was a small black car with purple-tinted windows. Having a car meant I could now travel further away in search of a higher-paying job.

Once I started to drive, I began to look for other places to work. My mother had a close connection with some of the women at Sliders, a nearby hamburger restaurant. They were interested in hiring, so I applied, interviewed, and got the job. The lady who interviewed me was named Mona, and I remember she had a gold tooth in the front of her mouth.

I was trained by some of the best employees Sliders had to offer, so I quickly learned a job. Donna, Rachael, Glenda, Theresa, Amos, and Johnetta all took me underneath their wings. There was a sense of camaraderie and teamwork at Sliders. The experience at Sliders was more intimate than my previous jobs and we worked in close quarters with one another. I got to know these people very well and vice-versa. There was a sense of humor and commonality that we all shared in common. I pulled pranks during work like hiding in the freezer and popping out surprising workers who walked by. They distributed paychecks weekly, gave free food to employees, and paid above the minimum wage. At Sliders, you could earn a raise every six months, which was also a nice benefit. I earned 18 cents on my first raise, taking my pay to $6.18. As a growing boy, I loved the fact that I could eat for free and took advantage of the opportunity to do so.

I also had an opportunity to use my Spanish speaking ability at Sliders. One day, I drove to work to pick up my paycheck. The payday was on Thursdays. I quickly noticed that they were five new employees behind the counter. They were five Guatemalan men and none of them could speak English. I remember the ladies working on the shift being very frustrated with the inability to communicate with the new employees. I saw this as an opportunity to show my highest potential and save the day. I went behind the counter and immediately started to speak Spanish to the men. I trained them on the fryer and the grill by translating how to operate the equipment. It was not complete training, but it was good enough that they could function within the fast-food restaurant that evening. I felt so good about the chance to highlight my skills and be an asset to my company.

I went home and told my mother about the experience, after picking up my check. I said to her *"Mom, today at work we had these Spanish men come in and nobody could talk to them, so I spoke Spanish and trained them on what to do!"* She replied, "That's nice son, but they need to pay you for that." The response from my mother caught me by surprise. For some reason, I was expecting her to be happier for me and my accomplishment. However, she was trying to teach me a lesson in self-worth, value, and business. My mother knew that I had many years attending foreign language academies and she didn't want me to be taken advantage of. She instructed me to not use my Spanish speaking ability unless I was being paid for it.

The next day when I reported to work, of course, all five men were working on my shift. The managers and employees were all smiling and relieved once I arrived. I asked the manager if I could speak to her for a second and she agreed. I told her exactly what my mother had told me to say. I reported, *"Miss Mona, I don't mind training these men, in fact, I enjoy doing it, but my mother said if I am going to be training them then I need to be paid for it."* The manager told me that wasn't a problem after consulting with the district manager. I was granted an extra dollar for each extra person that I was training on my shift. I had already earned eighteen cents on my first raise, so instead of making the starting wage of six dollars, I was making $6.18. The extra dollar for each of the men I was training increased my pay to $11.18. This was great money for a high school student. I could keep gas in my car, buy whatever clothes I wanted to, and buy gifts for birthdays and holidays. I continued to work at Sliders until it was time for me to exit for the military. Sliders was without a doubt the most enjoyable employment from my childhood.

Through my work experiences, I believe God was showing me the capacity of my brain and the value of an honest day's work. I enjoyed doing a good job and getting attention for standing out and being exceptional. I learned the importance of being on time, being professional, and giving my best effort. I was able to build up my confidence and grow social skills that became useful in my life. I have always been an asset to any company I have ever worked for. I am grateful for the people who went out of their way to teach me something along the way. I thank God for giving me a chance to use the skills and abilities He blessed me with.

Working at the Smart Lab

Chapter 13

Man of the House

"Trust in the Lord with all your heart, and do not lean on your own understanding. In all your ways acknowledge him, and he will make straight your paths." **Proverbs 3:5-6**

I have always known who my biological Dad was and have been told numerous times how much I look like him. My Dad was Uncle Eric, and everyone's favorite member of the family. My Dad loved his kids, but he was not the best husband to my Mother. There was only a small amount of time that I recall him living within my household. One night, I remember he woke me up out of my sleep and gave me some soda. At times, I remember him asking me to walk on his back. I had no idea what I was doing, but he seemed to enjoy the mere pressure from my body weight on his back. I would laugh as he moaned and groaned with each directed step he gave me.

I remember witnessing my Dad abusing my Mom when he stayed with us. One night, I was sleeping in my Mother's room and suddenly awakened by loud noises. I was scared and trembling, as I peeked through the covers while pretending to be asleep. I saw my Dad angrily mounted on top of my Mother and striking her. I can still see him repeatedly slapping and hitting my Mom, as she laid helpless in defense begging him to stop. I got up shortly after the violence was over and started crying. I remember my Mother doing her best to stay strong by uttering, "It will be okay, go back to sleep baby." I sobbed for my Mom that night, but I never felt in danger from my Dad personally. The memory still hurts, but that experience helped me understand why my Dad didn't stay with us.

Everyone has their cross to bear. The time my Dad spent away from us was heavily impacted by his hardcore drug use. My Dad was a heroin addict, but as a kid, I could never tell any difference in him. Unfortunately, the negative drug habit affected other members of the family as well. I do remember seeing him use a key to snort a few lines of a white powder in his nostril before, but his behavior towards me didn't change. Eric James Isaacs could do no wrong in my eyes when I was a child. He was loving towards me and I cherished every moment we spent together. I love and accept him for the good and the bad.

Although my Dad didn't stay with us, we would get to see him occasionally. Mainly, seeing my Dad was dependent on his ability to keep himself clean. He stayed with my Aunt Pat while living in Cincinnati and we would often visit him there. We had good times at Aunt Patty Jo's house and I enjoyed playing my Cousin Patrice's keyboard. My Dad called Patrice "Puddems," and I have called her the same ever since. During those times, he taught me some valuable lessons in manhood. Since I was the oldest boy, I had to learn how to become the man of the house.

First, my Dad made sure I understood that it was my responsibility to take care of my brothers. He did so one time, by reprimanding us for how we went up the steps during a visit with him. I sped up the steps first, followed by my brother Ricardo in a mad dash to the top of the stairs. He stopped us and corrected us about leaving our brother Rico behind. Rico was born physically handicap, so felt it was the other brother's job to protect him. He lined us up in the order he wanted us to go up the stairs, which had me in the back of the line. He put Rico in the middle of the line. Ricardo, was first to protect against anything from the front side. I understood the point he was making and took it to heart. I started to become a better brother and took more responsibility. I did my best to steer my brothers away from getting in trouble. I knew that if I got into trouble and did bad things, then they were going to follow my lead.

Another lesson my Dad taught me was about not being afraid in my own city. Papa was a rolling stone, so often I would accompany him to visit women in different neighborhoods. One time, he was visiting his lady friend in the heart of downtown Cincinnati. At this time, the neighborhood was considered very dangerous and I would have never been there at that hour if it were not for him. After leaving the lady's apartment, we walked in the neighborhood to a nearby family member's house. I reminisce being nervous and walking cautiously, which drew my Dad's attention. He declared to me, "These are *your* streets son, *you* are from here! You don't ever need to be afraid to walk on *your streets*." This experience was received as a lesson in manhood and courage. Subsequently, I was able to move around my city with *hometown confidence.*

The next lesson my Dad taught me was a punching combination. One weekend, I was hanging out with my Dad at my aunt's house and we were making breakfast. He made fried egg sandwiches and was explaining to me how to do it, too. I also remember him talking to me about dust mites and the harm they can cause. He instructed me to not leave silverware on the counter because dust mites were present on most surfaces. The lesson, however, was in what he taught me while the eggs were cooking. It was a quick punching combination that faked a body shot leading into a short hook. I practiced it over and over mimicking his every move. He pushed and encouraged me to master it. After much practice, I had the attack figured out. It became one of my signature punching combinations, and I have never forgotten it.

One evening, I was with my Dad at his barbershop and he asked me to go to the store for him. He gave me money and told me he wanted a ginger ale and some chips. My brother, another kid that was hanging out at the shop, and I safely crossed the street and went to the store to retrieve the items. When we arrived, a local drug dealer was talking loud to the owner and patrons within the establishment. I recognized him because we lived in the neighborhood and he was frequently hanging out on the street corners. At this time, there was an ice cream cooler in front of the store near the cash register area. I picked up the soda and chips my father had requested and proceeded to the cashier counter. The drug dealer was just leaving the store by the time I was ready to check out at the register.

As I approached the counter, there was a large wad of money laying on the freezer directly in front of me. The drug dealer had removed a wad of cash from his sock and placed it on the freezer, as he paid for his items. He must have forgotten that he had laid down the large sum of cash. I realized the money was left unclaimed and my heart started to pound beneath my chest. As I walked closer, a shining one hundred dollar bill was staring me in the face. Even though there was a wad of cash, the gleaming and glowing one hundred dollar bill had my undivided attention. The store attendant had not noticed the left behind money. I moved as close as I could to the ice cream cooler and slid the hundred in my pocket. I grabbed the remaining money and handed it over to the store owner as lost money. The store owner was an Arab man named Sam and he didn't hesitate to take the cash. As a kid, although I did steal the one hundred, it seemed like turning in the rest of the abandoned money was the right thing to do. I did not alert my brother about the mischievous deed. I hurried out of the store and we rushed back to my father's barbershop immediately.

Once I arrived at the barbershop and felt safe, I told my Dad about what happened during our trip to the store. I was fearful that the drug dealer would find out that I took the money, but my Dad was intrigued about the details and the least bit worried. He was actively listening to the story that I had told him. He had instantly recognized that there was an unclaimed lump sum of money that I last had possession of at the store. He took custody of the one hundred dollar bill, gathered a few items, and said, "Let's go, we are going back to the store!"

We headed back to the store and I remember being afraid and feeling like there were butterflies in my stomach. By the time we arrived at the store, the drug dealer had already returned and was into a lively confrontation with the store owner. The drug dealer was yelling "Nah Sam, that's my money and I have shit to do today, so you need to give me my money!" The store owner replied, "No, No, No, how much money are you missing?" The drug dealer escalated his voice, while emphatically clapping his hands saying, "I'm missing 450 dollars, Sam!" My Dad was listening intently and recognized that there were $350 dollars in the lost and found wad of cash. He already knew that I had the anonymous one hundred dollar bill.

Sam counted the money behind the register out of sight of the angry dealer. Sam stated, "No, there is not 450 dollars here." The dealer became extremely aggravated asserting, "That is my f*cking money, Sam!" My Dad kindly interrupted and asked Sam, "So you're telling me that if I can tell you how much money is in that stack you will give it to me?" The dealer looked back at my dad and wanted no parts of him, but adamantly protested his claim. I was scared of the drug dealer, but the dealer was much more afraid of the real gangster in the building. My Dad stayed laser-focused on Sam who seemed to be considering my Dad's offer. My Dad proclaimed,

"So, that could be anybody's money then." Before Sam could respond, the dealer pushed back maintaining, "Nah fuck that Sam, that's my f*cking money man!" Tensions rose as Sam seemed confused and unsure about what to do. Sam finally responded, "Well I will just have to report the turned in money to the police!" The dealer became enraged and stormed out of the store declaring he would be coming back for his money. My dad let some time go by before trying to persuade the owner again. By this time, the store owner had made up his mind that he was turning the money over to the police. More than likely he kept it to himself.

I admired my Dad's courage, status, and confidence in the situation. It was a scary situation for me, but he was calm, collected, and calculated in his approach. I well understood why my Dad earned the nickname "Cool Breeze." He also taught me a valuable lesson that day about street credibility. I had no idea who my father was on the street, but I realized that day that he was fearless and respected.

My Dad decided to hold onto the one hundred dollars for me. When I went home, I told my Mother about the day's events and my having possession of one hundred dollars. My Mother asked me where the money was and I told her dad was holding it for me. She immediately called my Dad and demanded that he handed the money over to me. I didn't understand why she was so upset when I was younger. Looking back at the situation, I can see that my Mom was well aware of my Dad's drug habit. She insisted that the money was returned and it was. When my Dad gave me the money, he stated to me, "I was not going to keep *your* money son." I most definitely gave him the benefit of the doubt.

Around this time, I was heavily involved in church, so I had made the decision to pay my tithes with the money I had. I wanted to pay my ten percent as the bible instructs people to do. However, I was advised by my Grandma that children were not to pay adult prices, so I was giving away too much money paying ten. She told me to, "Just give five dollars and that's enough." I wish I had the courage to have stuck to my convictions, but I listened to her advice and paid five dollars. I still felt good about contributing to tithes and offerings with my own money, stolen or not. The rest of the one hundred dollars was spent on toys, such as action figures, a ring for my wrestling men, and a video game.

My Dad also taught me a thing or two about women. I remember him having great style and the importance he placed on being clean, neat, and fashionable. He also showed me how to see a girl's beauty beyond her face. As a kid, a girl being pretty was simply determined by how cute she was in the face. That was the standard I used to pick girlfriends during my elementary years. One time, while at the barbershop, my Dad was giving me a haircut in between waiting for his customers. A girl walked by on the sidewalk, but she did not initially get my attention. My dad asked me, "What do you think about that girl, Eric?" I gazed at her briefly and alleged, "*She's ugly!*" He laughed hysterically and questioned, "What makes her ugly to you son?" I indicated to him, "*Her face and she has a jerry curl.*" He continued to laugh and pronounced, "Forget her face son, and look at her legs!" Right then, I could see her full potential and it altered my perspective on a girl's beauty. From that day forward, I began to notice all of the beautiful parts and elements on a woman's exterior.

I remember going to Alabama and Florida with my Dad at the age of ten for two weeks. The first week was spent in Alabama, and the following week we traveled to Florida. We rode in a large blue family-sized van with one of my dad's friends to Birmingham, Alabama. I remember riding down the highway in the backseat of a van and being impressed with the sunset as it illuminated the horizon. This was the first time I remember traveling outside of the city of Cincinnati. Alabama was also the first place I saw my dad do a line of cocaine. As a child, I didn't understand what was going on because his love for me was constant.

While in Alabama, we stayed with a man by the name of Mr. Green. He was a tall man with a tapered afro and a goatee. I remember him because his house was painted in vivid green color, so much so that large water-bugs dwelled on the sides of the house mistaking it for grass. Mr. Green is the man who taught me how to play chess and is responsible for introducing me to the mental concept of thinking three moves ahead. He did not take it easy on me and that allowed me to learn and improve quickly. In chess, the best way to learn is to play with others that are more advanced than you. I never forgot how to play and passed the game on along to other family members.

Mr. Green had a mean Chow-Chow dog named Duke and a cat named Sampson. Duke was a guard dog and Sampson was a guard cat. You could not run in the yard because Duke was trained to attack anybody that ran. If any of the water-bugs made it inside the house, the cat would pounce on them and eat them. I noticed for the first time one night while sitting in the living room. I was watching the television and all of a sudden, I saw the cat dart quickly towards the door. I wonder what happened, but a loud "Crunch" sound ensued. I asked my dad about it and he said it was the cat's job. Duke and Sampson got along well and would sit on the front porch together during sunset. They both were working animals with specific jobs and they would relax on the porch after a hard day's work. He also had piranhas in the living room.

My Dad taught me how to fry pork chops using a deep fryer during that stay as well. I remember that being the first place I saw a dead dog on the side of the main road. It was some sort of black and white mutt and it was as stiff as a doorknob. I recall going to the projects with my Dad and meeting a kid named Bo. He was nice to me and ended up becoming a friend, at least for that week. He gave me three kittens upon returning from Florida. I gathered them in a box and fed them milk. When I came back home to Cincinnati, my mother would not let me keep any of the cats. I was willing to take care of them and had bonded with the kittens, but she was having no parts of it. She despises them as she does most animals.

The second week my Dad and I traveled to Florida and it was my very first time being on an airplane. I remember my ears popping and staring out the window in excitement and amazement. Once we landed, I recall meeting up with a dark-skin woman and her daughter. Their names evade me, but we stayed at her house during the time in Florida and the lady was our sponsor for the trip. She financed the entire expedition to Florida, as well as the festivities included. Her daughter was much younger than I and was fairly annoying throughout the vacation. I did my best to get along with her and ignore her obnoxiousness. We still had a great time though. We went everywhere in Orlando, including Disney World, Epcot Center, and Universal Studios. I remember everything being extremely expensive, but my dad convinced the woman to provide us with every amenity. It was one of the best experiences of my childhood because it was one-on-one time with my Dad. My Grandma Sarah once said to me that my Dad could "talk himself out of going to hell." My Dad was handsome, charming, charismatic, and comfortable around women. I believe that those qualities are inherently embedded in me as well.

One day, I recollect my Mother screaming out loud as I had never heard before. My brother and I ran downstairs to see what was going on. My Mother and sister were sobbing uncontrollably. My Mom screeched out "No, no, no!" and I asked her, "*What's the matter?*" She sharply replied, "Your daddy is dead!" It did not fully register, but I did my best to keep it calm because my mother and sister were hysterical. I was in shock still and could not believe the news I had just received. I cried privately, but there was something inside of me that knew I needed to be strong while my family members grieved. I was mad at him for leaving me and those sentiments postponed my tears.

I had feelings of sadness for not having my Dad for the rest of my life. I did not understand why God had taken my dad away from me? I did not know who would defend me or teach me the valuable lessons of manhood. My youth made me numb from the trauma, impact, and consequences of this loss in my life. I cried out to God and pleaded, "*What am I going to do?*" His response was, "*I am your father!*" I was hurt and didn't understand my feelings, but my spirit gave me comfort that things would be alright.

At my Dad's funeral, there were tons of familiar faces and several unfamiliar ones as well. I recognized my family members because my Dad made a point of bringing me around them. They had no explanation for his death, but they did their best to comfort me during the time. Many of them checked on me and I pretended to be fine, but I wasn't. I redirected the trauma by supporting my Mom, sister, and brothers. My sister wanted to take a final picture of my Dad from the casket, but I protested to her capturing the memory. However, I could not escape the memory of my Dad being lowered in his casket or lowered in his grave. I could not evade the fact that my Dad was gone and he was not coming back.

Soon after, my Aunt Gail and Uncle Vernie had passed away as well. It was all in a short amount of time, so the losses devastated my Dad's side of the family. During my childhood, at times I felt like they had abandoned me after my Dad's death. They were mourning and understandably so, but I really felt a distance between them during my grieving process. However, my relationships with my Aunt Patty Jo and my Uncle Stewart were always steady and consistent throughout my childhood. My Aunt Patty Jo would call and send gifts on our birthdays or

Christmas. She would also show up at my Mom's salon to see us and attended events. My Uncle Stewart would also call and I would spend time with him at his body shop in Avondale. He always talked to me like an Uncle and tried to share wisdom and stories about the family with me. He was the closest thing I had to my Dad, so I embraced every moment we had.

One of the unfamiliar faces was a guy that I learned was nicknamed, "Rock." I remember him because he was shaking profusely when he visited my dad's casket and I asked who he was. My aunt Gail yelled out, "Sit him down!" She then answered my question by whispering to me that was my dad's friend Rock. There were tons of others that I did not know, but a multitude of people attended his service. I also remember my Uncle Tony gave me a watch that belonged to my Dad.

I was familiar with the pastor, so that made the service a little easier to bear. It was Bishop O'Neil, who had grown up with my Dad, was my sister Tera's teacher, and an active member of the community. Several people were crying and I remember shedding some tears when Bishop O'Neil sang and when they closed the casket. He was singing a sacred gospel song called "I Won't Complain." He and his wife, Pastor Linda, sang heartfelt songs to comfort the family in our time of bereavement. The song is unforgettable because of the emotion and moment attached to it. I remember tearing up during the singing, however, the lasting impact of losing my Dad had not settled in yet.

I went through feeling resentment towards my dad, but I was also thankful for the time I had with him. At some point, I'm sure I questioned God wondering why my Dad had been taken from me at such an early age. However, God gave me a formula for accepting his death and becoming a man. That formula was to keep the good, drop the bad, and add some new. I kept the enduring qualities that made my dad special and loved; his love for his family, his gift of gab, and his laughter. I dropped the hard drug habits, the infidelity, and the abuse I witnessed my mother suffer from. Last, I let God add the new to create the man he wanted me to be.

My mother married Creester around the time Rico came home to live from the hospital. He met my Mom one day at the hospital while she was visiting with Rico. In a short amount of time, Creester had become my Step-Dad for many years of my childhood. Creester liked Prince and Eddie Murphy as entertainers. We had a big-screen television downstairs that no one was allowed to use but him. He had codes on the television and we only got to watch it a few times on special occasions. He had a loud and distinctive laugh. Creester was a good provider and did make the household feel safer with a man now in it. I appreciated that he took me to several of my practices, while my Mother was at work.

Creester wasn't a bad person, but I do feel like he tried to suppress us, boys. At times, he seemed to find amusement in our displeasure or misfortunes. I felt like he wanted me to be more submissive rather than build me to be strong and confident. He more or less did his best to keep me in check and exert his authority. Nonetheless, I am thankful for Creester because he was better than not having any male figure at all. Creester and my Mom eventually divorced after many years together, and I remember having feelings of abandonment when he left. More than anything, what I can say for Creester is that he was present in my childhood, and he gets credit for that.

When my Dad passed away, my uncle Topper really stepped up and developed a close bond with me. He would talk to me about boy issues and keep me in check when I was out of line. Uncle Topper is the person who defined the role of an uncle for me. He kept the conversation and relationship real with me at all times. He advised me about girls, the game, and fashion. He would let me drive sometimes and would do donuts in his car when it snowed. The ride in the spinning car felt like a roller coaster to me and I was thrilled. My Uncle Topper and I shared the same kind of style in clothing and liked the same kind of music. I remember Topper coming over to my house to raid my closet several times. I didn't mind because it made me feel like I had something important that was worth having. Topper was the all-time greatest uncle of my childhood. He loved me with everything he had and checked on me often.

Another family member who had an impact on my childhood was my uncle Charles. He was with my Aunt Debbie and is the dad of CJ, Woe, and Shaq. He had his own drug issues, but he was an amazing person and uncle to me consistently. My cousins were young when he was around, but I was old enough to remember who he was and what he did for me. He was the uncle that actually spent quality time and took care of us boys. He took us to the park to play, to the courts for practice, and to the fields to throw around the ball. He was also the first person to take me fishing. We would go to Burnet Woods and catch bluegill in the murky water. He was active in my childhood and a loving uncle regardless of blood relation. I will always have a love for Charles because of the care he provided to me as a kid.

Two other men who had positive impacts on my life during adolescence were Anthony and Irving. They were both my Mother's boyfriends at different times during my teenage years. Anthony was down to Earth and able to relate to me during some troubling times. He was non-judgmental and supportive of my views. I remember Anthony came to one of my high school football games against his former high school. He played basketball with me and was easy to talk to, but I did pick up his bad habit of smoking Black and Mild cigars. He didn't encourage me to, but I definitely did learn how to prepare or "freak" them by watching him. Irving was an ex-military guy, so he was stern but he gave me some useful advice that later paid dividends. He advised me to take a sewing class my senior year even though I opposed it initially. I remember him saying to me, "Take the class; you never know when you might use the skill in the future." I am glad I did heed the advice.

Tera's boyfriend Tez came later during my adolescent years, but he was welcomed with open arms. He was a large man I watched him on the football field at Aiken before he started dating my sister. He was nice to me from the first time I met him and he always wore some Nike Cortez shoes. I admired him and for the first time, it felt like I had a big bro. He would drive me places in his long white vehicle, which had booming speakers in the back. Riding with him was the first time I hear UGK's *Riding Dirty*. I felt much safer when Tez joined our family because I felt like some of the pressure to be the man of the house was not solely on me.

Overall, I am thankful for the men who did invest time and energy into my upbringing. Whether good or bad, I used the men as examples in my formative years. Having a Dad and a Stepdad temporarily was better than having nothing at all. Ultimately, God wanted no man before him in my life. When I needed something or prayed for something, I prayed to Jesus and he always answered my call. He was there for me when no one else was and it was Him that was protecting me all along.

Dad and I

Chapter 14

Paramours

"Little children, let us not love in word or talk but in deed and in truth." **1 John 3:18**

I had my first girlfriend by kindergarten, and her name was Cassie. I remember she was beautiful and flat out gorgeous to me. She was a light-skinned, curly-haired mixed girl with a beautiful smile and the most adorable dimples. In fact, she was my girlfriend all the way up until the fourth grade. She was easily the most admired girl in my grade level. She left our school in fourth grade when her mother moved and put her into a different school system. It may not seem like much, but any relationship beyond two weeks in grade school is a big deal. Being able to stay boyfriend and girlfriend from kindergarten to fourth grade was very much a relationship. She was pretty and nice to me, which is all I required at such a young age. At the beginning of each school year, I would go up to her and ask, "Are you still my girlfriend?" Nothing delighted and reassured me more than when she would flash me that dazzling smile and respond, "Yes!"

I remember one time going to her house for a birthday party. Her mother didn't like me at all. She would look at me with her nose raised and automatically thought I was in trouble. I believe she was more concerned that her daughter was head over heels in love with some black kid from the projects. There were a few of the kids from school that attended the party, but Cassie showed me the most attention and interest that day.

At one point during the free-play portion of the party, Cassie took me to her room and closed the door. I was worried about getting in trouble, but Cassie was unafraid of the consequences. She was not the least bit concerned, so I followed her energy and went into the bedroom together. I was a little scared, but she assured me that everything would be fine and it was her room. I remember one kid, Ryan, came by and knocked on the door while we were in there. He was standing outside of the door knocking to get in. We knew it was just another kid, so we dashed and hid in the closet. In that closet is where I experienced my first kiss. It was an amazing thrill for me as a young boy. Here I was, five or six years old and already on first base.

I savored the moment for several seconds and then we exited the closet, motioning towards the door. I was afraid that Ryan's knocking had already alerted the adults at the party. However, Cassie dared me not to open it, so I stopped in my tracks and focused my attention back on her. She had on a pretty pink dress and some stockings. I told her how beautiful she was and she kindly accepted my compliments. She asked me to come and sit on her bed and I did. We sat on the bed and I asked her the oddest question, which was "Can I see your feet?" She agreed to let me, but her facial expression showed she was trying to figure out why in the world I wanted to see her feet. I admit, it was a bit weird and I couldn't tell you exactly why I requested permission from her to see her feet. No, I didn't have some kind of weird foot fetish or anything. The best way to explain this request is, it allowed me access to her like no other boy was allowed before. No one had ever laid eyes on Cassie's feet, so I was determined to be the first boy to do so. Cassie took her dress sandals off and I took a peek at her small, petite foot. Shortly after that, we left the room and rejoined the party. It is hilarious to think back on how childish my mind worked at the time.

I also remember one time in first grade, we were allowed some free time at the end of class. A group of us students gathered in the back of the classroom behind the easel. There were several students in the classroom, so the teachers' attention was divided among the other students. I was in the group with Cassie and a girl named Blair. Blair was a good friend, who was extremely smart and could fluently read and write in the first grade. Somehow, she had gotten ahold of a sexually-explicit book and was reading it to the group of students behind the easel. We all formed a close circle and Cassie and I were wedged in the middle. From the teacher's perspective, what we were doing may have seemed innocent. Whenever she came near, Blair would read from one of the more generic portions of the book. She had a book cover on the book, so the teacher had no idea what was going on. In actuality, Cassie and I were in the middle of the circle hugging and kissing, acting out the scenes as Blair narrated.

Once Cassie left our school, I had no choice but to be thrown out into the open waters of the adolescent dating pool. After the booming relationship with Cassie, I dated a few girls who had liked me for a while. One girl was a friend named Yachika. She had big lips, but she was nice to me and would bring me candy. That lasted for a few weeks before I broke up with her. I had the bright idea of trying to date a girl from the grade level above me, named Anetra. She was a slender, dark-skinned girl with beautiful hazel eyes. She was much more aggressive than I was used to. She was popular, loud, and had my attention because she rode my bus. She did become my girlfriend, but that relationship may have made it a couple of weeks.

From my lens, I had several meaningful relationships with girls throughout my childhood. One day at football practice, I gained the attention of the Captain of the cheerleaders for my team. Her name was Tamika. She was popular within her own right and definitely elevated my status among my peers. Back then, Tamika was the girl that all the guys raved about. She was fun, an excellent dancer, and had a body beyond her years. She was a brown-skinned girl with beautiful facial features and the nicest butt of all. Before I knew who she was, I would hear my teammates mention her name when talking about the cutest cheerleaders. She was full of personality, sexiness, and sass.

Tamika admired me for what she witnessed me doing on the football field and I admired her for how she led the cheerleaders. We were so in love that we would look at one another during the games. She frequented Golden Skates and her and I would bump and grind more than a few times throughout the evening. We both treated each other well during our relationship and exchanged gifts during holidays and birthdays. I remember her mother was one of the bus drivers at the top of the hill, so Tamika would pass gifts and messages through her sometimes. Her mother knew I was a good kid and I'm sure she thought our little relationship was funny and cute. One additional perk to dating Tamika was that she had a younger sister, Tina, who cheered for my brother's team. Tina and Ricardo eventually became a couple as well.

Tamika and I were committed to one another for a considerable amount of time during my adolescence. I trusted her and she made me feel like she was genuinely interested in me. We would both show each other tons of affection whenever we were near. Often, we exchanged hugs, touches, and long kisses on the lips. I held her attention for a long time, but she was much more advanced than me.

Tamika's family moved to my neighborhood and I was happy she was staying close to me. However, our relationship quickly began to turn as soon as she moved in. Tamika became distant and ignored my phone calls for a couple of days. By the time I did get in contact with her, Tamika had already become popular and familiar with the other boys in the neighborhood. At that particular time, I did not know how to meet all of her physical needs. I could not prevent the older boys from pursuing her the way she desired. I was hurt and it broke my young heart, but I couldn't be mad at her. She was an excellent girlfriend to me for years and was always honest with me about everything. Even when Tamika was ready to move on, she was honest about it and told me.

It hurt my feelings when I could no longer please her, but I left that relationship with a lot of dating experiences. I learned some valuable lessons from the relationship with Tamika that I carried into the future. Trust, commitment, and honesty to be specific. I learned that you should tell someone the truth even if it hurts their feelings. Yes, it saddened me initially when Tamika said that it was over, but it also allowed for me to have closure.

After that, I began to date a girl from school named Keisha. She was the Black Stallion, dark-skinned, with a beautiful smile, and a figure comparable to Tamika. She had an older sister I knew from school that I got along with as well. Keisha set her eyes on becoming my girlfriend and we were dating before I even knew what happened. I could never forget the bus rides home that year. Keisha and I rode the same bus and we both would always sit in the back seats. With my jacket covering our heads, we would kiss and feel on each other the whole ride home. The time I spent practicing with Keisha taught me how to touch a girl. She placed my hands where she wanted them and I learned how she liked to be touched. Keisha taught me how to round second base. We dated for the middle of the year and broke up towards the end of the school year.

After my relationship with Keisha, I experienced a series of random short-term relationships with girls from my classrooms, my neighborhood, or the grade level above me. I remember one of those girls who was named Tory. I had known her since Mt. Airy and she was a pretty and popular girl with tons of personality. She was always nice to me and the relationship lasted a few weeks, which is standard for most middle school flings. Most of the connections were brief in time as I transitioned to a different school, Finneytown.

Finneytown had a much different demographic than I was familiar with. With the majority of the girls being white, I set my eyes on the pretty ones first. I soon learned that dating a white girl was much different than the girls I had previously dated. My normal methods for gaining the attention and interest of a young lady were ineffective. The dating game for me had changed and evolved into an unfamiliar realm, but that did not stop me from trying.

I struck out on the first few popular girls I attempted to date. I ended up settling on a girl named Brittany. She was sociable, available, and agreed to be my girlfriend. I knew better than to let my mother find out I was dating a white girl. Without a doubt, my mother had prejudice towards white women dating black men. She would tell me whenever a white girl was brought up, "*You better not bring no white bitch to my house!*" She would say it jokingly, but I took the warning seriously. However, my uncle Topper had been dating white girls for as long as I can remember. Although my Mom had her own prejudices, I was not afraid to date whoever I liked. I knew I would not be the first person in the family to bring a white girl home.

I feared how she would react when a formal dance was being held at the school, and I planned on taking a white girl. She wasn't thrilled about it, to say the least, but she still allowed me to go to the dance with Brittany. However, once Brittany's mother found out she was going to the dance with a black kid, her mother decided to cancel the date altogether. My mother used that action by Brittany's mother to support her claims on interracial dating. I left the Finneytown district and went to a new school for 9th grade.

Early on in high school, I set my sights high and sought to gain the interest of a beautiful girl named Rachael. She was a popular girl, smart, and was an aspiration for the boys in my grade level. She made it obvious and clear to me that she was interested in me by flashing me her flattering and gentle smile. She had a great sense of humor and was very intelligent. We had a great connection and would have a stimulating conversation during phone calls. Rachael was the first girl I fell in love with in high school; I felt important whenever she gave me her undivided attention. I found her interesting and committed myself exclusively to her in our relationship.

We dated for a nice length of time during the ninth grade year until she played me for an upperclassman named Assa. Unfortunately, Rachael is most memorable for being the first girl in high school to break my heart. I had all the best intentions for my relationship, but I was caught off guard and negatively affected by the deception. When I found out, Rachael was kind of cold and remorseless about it. This event sent me into a slight spiral and I too became more cold and heartless. I made the decision to protect myself at all cost and never let another girl hurt my feelings so deeply. I stopped wearing my heart on my shoulder and started to look out for my own best interest no matter what in relationships. I still treated my girlfriends with respect, but I started to look out for myself above all else.

My next girlfriend was initially my rebound girl but eventually became much more. The girl happened to be a tenth grader by the name of Christina. She was a smart girl and had a cool personality, so those qualities overshadowed whatever she may have lacked in the look department. She was definitely not an ugly girl and I was attracted to her physically. I thought she was pretty and I was mesmerized by her piano playing ability. She rode my bus and every day after school, she would invite people over to her house. At these gatherings, we would play music, clown, socialize, and most of all get our freak on. Soon after, I asked Christina to be my girlfriend and she said, "Yes". I was taught how to turn the corner on third base at these parties.

Body parts came into play as my body had developed well into puberty. That was the first time I got to see girls topless and witnessed the aftermath of a boy getting too excited while grinding with a girl. A boy and a girl would go into the bedroom or an isolated area during a song. The girls would show us their breasts and allow us to touch them freely. The girls were permitted to touch and explore the boys however they wanted to. The boys and girls would switch every few songs, but I would focus most of my time and attention on Christina. She was my girlfriend during that time and I didn't want her to catch feelings of jealousy. One of my buddies went in the closet with a thick legged beauty and he was wearing light green jogging pants. After several minutes, he came out of the closet with a dark green stain around his private area.

I loved the access I had to Christina, but also how she had patience in teaching me things. She was the first girl to show me the benefit of playing music during alone time with a partner. Christina gave me access to her body like I never experienced before. At one of those parties at her house, Christina also taught me how to lose my virginity. She pulled me into the back room and laid me on the bed. She pulled out her breast for me to play with and let me suck on them. I was definitely aroused to my fullest at this point. Christina straddled me and began to grind on top of me. Shortly after that, she gave me a condom and I put it on as I had learned in previous sex education classes. With me on my back, I slid right inside her and didn't have to worry about finding it. Those magical moments lasted all of maybe three minutes, but I remember it vividly like it was yesterday.

The first time I ejaculated, I remember feeling like my life had changed. All of a sudden things had started to make sense. That which was misunderstood all of a sudden felt connected and in place. Christina and I continued to date, but we eventually broke up and went our separate ways. By the time we broke up, I had gained the attention of the girls I really wanted to pursue. Christina did a great job of advertising me as a boyfriend by bragging to all of her friends about how well I treated her. Consequently, I became aware of several other girls who were interested in me, as my social circle increased.

I began dating Delilah in the second half of my ninth-grade year. She was friends with Christina, and I learned of who she was through the after school parties. She was a bubbly, intelligent, and extremely positive dark-skinned beauty. She was a church-going girl and that was attractive to me as well because I was also raised in the church. Delilah attending one of Christina's after school parties were how I learned that she liked to have fun. She had a distinctive laugh, a cute smile, and a spirit about her that I found adorable. She was a joyful and positive person to be around. Although my heart was jaded at the time, Delilah always recognized and encouraged the best qualities in me. She was a little more sheltered than I was used to, but she was sociable with lots of energy for life.

We grew closer and Delilah became an important person in my young life. She showed me an unconditional love like I had not experienced in relationships before. She accepted me for who I was and found humor in my mistakes. Delilah was likable, easy-going, and always caring towards me. Even in times where I might have done something wrong towards her, Delilah could express it to me lovingly, so I could consider it. She made it easy for me to love her and I reciprocated her interest and feelings. I was trustworthy and had no doubt in my mind that she was faithful during our relationship. We adored each other and were able to build love and affection in our relationship. I spoiled her by bringing large gifts to school for Valentine's Day and other special occasions. It was my job to make sure she smiled each day and do something funny so I could enjoy her laughter.

Delilah was the first girl I took to church with my family. We talked on the phone every day engaging in intimate conversations. Delilah's mother was a hairstylist just like my mother. Her father was a fire-fighter and he didn't like me from the start. I don't think I had much chance with him and it had nothing to do with me. His daughter was head over heels for me, so he did his best to intimidate me. It was not nearly as enough needed to keep me away from Delilah. I liked everything about her and how she treated me. She helped build my confidence during our relationship and complimented me on how charming and sweet I was often.

I knew Delilah was a virgin, and the fact that no other boy could say they were with her sexually meant something to me. I respected her wishes to postpone sex, but quite honestly my hormones were in overdrive during my high school years. However, her wanting to take things slowly did not stop me from falling for her. We would talk about sex sometimes and she eventually became more comfortable with the idea. I had more experiences than her at the time, so I felt there was still plenty for her to learn from me. I portrayed as if I had no worries and life all figured out, but truly I didn't. I was still actively involved in learning myself.

We had a great relationship until I messed it up at the end of our freshman year. It all started when we had a school dance called Frosh. Delilah was my date, but I wasn't driving yet, so the plan was for us to meet up at the event location. I rode with Matt, my buddy from school, and the neighborhood. I danced with several people during the night, but I gave Delilah the overwhelming portion of my time once she arrived. We had a great time and enjoyed ourselves the entire night. The plan was for Delilah and me to meet at the dance, and her father had volunteered to escort us home.

After the dance was over, everyone filed into the parking lot socializing and finding their rides. The students were all discussing which restaurant we were going to meet up at. Her father drove a large black SUV at the time. I opened the door and there he was with a scowl in his eyebrows above his sunglasses. There were other people in the truck as well, which I was not expecting. However, I welcomed the additional company because it took some of the heat off of me. Delilah was sitting in the second row to the back. I entered the truck and sat in the last seat in the backseat of the truck. This put me next to Alice, which was a friend of both Delilah and me.

Alice was a full-figured, beautiful, light-skinned girl with long curly hair. She kind of had an exotic look about her and was very funny, so got along well. Delilah's father watched me for most of the ride home through the rearview mirror, with his eyes piercing through his shades. I sat away from Delilah to ease his concerns, but that would not satisfy him. He drove us to get something to eat and then proceeded to take us home.

All of the kids in the truck were excited and talking about the evening's dance. I was leaning forward from the rear seat engaging in conversation with the rest of the group. Unexpectedly, Alice began to gently caress the inside of my leg. This immediately got my attention and arousal. I pretended not to notice but began to reciprocate the touching as we all continued in conversation as if nothing was going on. I knew what was going on was wrong, but I didn't stop what was happening. It wasn't my mind or my heart, but my private part and hormones making the decision for me. She continued to stroke my leg upwards and I moved my hand towards her leg, giving her permission for me to explore.

The backseat escapade intensified very quickly. I can remember struggling to restrain my responses from the physical action. Alice was pressing all the right buttons and I had no defense for her offense. We stopped for a second, but our hormones were raging out of control. I thought it was over and that I had resisted the temptation, but I had clearly underestimated the moment. I looked up and Delilah's father was still watching me. He was clueless though as to what was going on beneath his view in the backseat. I continued in conversation with the group to distract and disguise what had just occurred.

All of sudden, Alice pulled on my right sleeve, dropping it from the seat in front of us where Delilah was sitting. Alice took control of my hand once it was out of view. She placed my hand on her leg and led it underneath her dress. I could feel the heat and warmth on my fingertips. I began to finger her and I could notice it being harder for her to restrain herself. She was squinting, biting her lip, and groaning underneath the noise in the vehicle. I knew what was going on was wrong, but because Alice initiated the deed, I honestly thought no one would find out.

I continued until we ran out of time on the ride. She let me know she climaxed by twitching, squeezing my hand, and then laying still afterward in bliss. I snuck in a sniff of my fingers and they were as fresh as water. We both transitioned back into the socialization seamlessly without anybody recognizing what had just happened. I was dropped off and exited the vehicle unaware of any consequences that would follow.

The next day of school following the dance, the rumors had already begun to spread prior to my arrival. Alice had felt guilty about what happened because she was friends with Delilah. Alice and I were friends as well, so I expected her to protect me. However, Alice felt the need to confess her mistake and clear her conscience. Unfortunately, the news was circulated socially and it led to me breaking Delilah's heart. It is not something I am proud of, but it happened and I felt horrible about it after. I was busted for cheating, but I mainly was upset about how I mistreated Delilah. She definitely did not deserve it and was one of the best girlfriends I ever had.

Delilah and I broke up by default from the news going around, but we remained close throughout high school. I had a lot of making up to do, but we eventually did get back together for a considerable amount of time. One day, Delilah provoked me into coming to visit her at her house. She assured me that we would be alone because her parents were at work. I arrived at her house and Delilah answered the door wearing nothing but a robe. Underneath the robe, she was completely nude and gracefully guided me to her bedroom. Delilah gave me her virginity that day at her house. The moment was filled with passion, but it did not last very long. I remember being worried and distracted by the thought of her father showing up. It still was special because of the bond we had established, and the fact that she had chosen to share herself with me in this way. Delilah and I always had respect, positive regard, and admiration for one another. We dated off and on after that, but I consider her my first true love in high school.

Ruby was a little younger than I, but somehow made her way into my social circle. I had a buddy who mentioned her prior to me meeting her. I think he may have even liked her at that time. However, from the first time I saw Ruby, we had similar attitudes and personalities. She made it obvious to me that she was interested in me. She was a sexy, short, mocha-skin color, and top-heavy. Ruby gained my attention because she was ambitious, silly, and determined to be around me whenever possible. She also loved sports, which made our conversations easy on the telephone. Ruby liked the same teams and players as I did. We both were die-heart Cincinnati sports fans, especially for the Bengals. Without much effort, Ruby and I became friends and began spending time together. We shared many laughs together because we both had the same sense of humor. We repeated famous lines from movies and thought each other's interpretations were hilarious.

Ruby and I got to know each other better but didn't make our relationship official at first. We first became friends by talking during hallway transitions at certain times during the school day and talk on the telephone. She was a virgin when we first met, but she was much more ready and prepared to offer hers to me. She had already made the decision on her own that I was going to be the person she would have her first experience with. One day after school, she asked me if I would take her home. I agreed and drove to her house. She asked me if I wanted to come in and I asked her if it was safe. Ruby confirmed her mother was at work and it was perfectly safe to enter, so I agreed. She opened the door and immediately led me to her room. She started playing some music, so she and I started kissing and taking clothes off. This was my first time really having any four-play involved. I took my time and made love to the whole Donnell Jones album. It was a great experience for us both and we made our relationship official afterward. It went so well that we planned to do it again, a short time after.

The following time we hooked up after school, it began much like the first time. However, the mood was set this time by R. Kelly's album and the result was much different. Ruby and I started to remove our clothes and began to engage in four-play. Prior to us getting into the act, we both heard a loud screech of tires from outside the window. The sound must have been familiar because Ruby quickly got up, wrapped in the blanket, and glanced out the window. Next thing I know,

I hear Ruby say, "Ah shit!" I immediately asked her what was wrong and she cried, "My momma just came home!"

I instantly went into a panic mode, got my shirt on, and hid in the closet. I threw the condom to Ruby and told her to "Get rid of it!" Her mother entered the home and already had an inclination about what was going on. She came up the stairs shouting, "What are doing home so early, Ruby?" Ruby was doing her best to make up excuses about why she was home earlier than usual. Her mother was not buying her story and continued to charge her way closer to Ruby's room. Her mother interrogated, "Who are you in here with Ruby?" Ruby claimed "Nobody." I was well hidden in the closet behind some clothes, but my legs and socks could be seen in the rear of the closet. I could hear her mother enter the room as she immediately checked in the closet where I was hiding. She stepped on my foot to let me know I was busted and I came out with my hands up.

I was so nervous and scared about being caught. She brought me down to the kitchen, and I nervously requested a glass of water. She poured a cup and handed it to me as I sat at the table. The mother told me to call my mother. I was staying with my sister at the time, so I called her apartment and my brother-in-law received the call. He came and picked me up, and had a conversation with Ruby's mom about what happened. I apologized and then exited making my way back home. My brother in law could not condemn my action as another male, but he did emphasize that I needed to get permission from the girls' parents before entering their home.

Ruby and I continued to date for a while. Her mother actually knew I was a good kid and she liked me, so she did not disapprove of Ruby and I seeing each other. From that point forward, anytime I wanted to see Ruby, I simply asked permission to come over when her mom was present. Her mother and I found a healthy and mutual respect for one another. Even after we eventually broke up, Ruby and I remained good friends throughout school. She was without a doubt one of my closest female companions.

Yasmin was another girl that I was familiar with from school. She was pretty, smart, and had a mystique about the way she carried herself. She was highly sought after by many of my peers and was more introverted than any other girl I had been around. I gained her interest by being persistent and a gentleman. One day, she came into the local grocery store where I worked. I noticed her and was happy to see her come and stand in my lane for service. As the cashier, that day I made her smile and I'm sure I left a great impression on her. Anytime I got an opportunity to be in her presence, I would take advantage of it and pursue her there. She eventually opened up to me and allowed me access to get to know her. Yasmin was going through a lot of emotional issues at home, so with her, I learned how to listen to a girl.

Over time, we developed an emotional bond and affection for each other. We had physical contact with one another at times, but we never had sex. Our relationship was based on trust and spending quality time together. Yasmin had no problem with whatever I did when I was away from her, but she expected her individualized time consistently. I loved to make her laugh and take her on spontaneous adventures around the city. Yasmin thought my antics were hilarious, but she had a serious side as well. I did not consider her my girlfriend because we never made it official or had sex, but in Yasmin's mind, we were very much in a relationship. When she found out I thought of her solely as a friend, she was hurt and refused to talk to me for years. She taught a lesson about the wrath of a woman's scorn.

During my high school years, I watched many episodes of the television show Martin. Martin Lawrence had a huge influence on the type of comedy I pursued. I was impacted by his physical and expressive way of being funny. Martin's girlfriend in the show was named Gina. She was a big head light-skinned girl, but I found her extremely attractive. She was likely the muse I used as a reference for a girlfriend. Gina was beautiful in my eyes and she became my preference when it came to girls. She was my ideal woman. The one I saw myself falling in love with and committing to. My Gina was named Monique and we were in a relationship for a large amount of time in high school. She was fairly quiet and unknown to me prior to meeting her.

One day at football practice, my friend Jay had called her over. He was interested in her and engaged her in conversation. Nothing against Jay, but I knew Monique was going to be my girlfriend from the moment I laid eyes on her. The first time I saw her I was blown away and thought she was stunning. Monique was everything I desired to have in a girlfriend. She was adorable and had an angelic vibe about her. She too was raised in the church while growing up and had a relationship with God. Monique was reserved and that attracted me to her even more. There was something special to me about a girl that everyone in school had not already dated. Monique did not pay me much attention at that first encounter and she was not impressed at all by us being on the football field. She offered something different in a girl than I had experienced before. She was my dream girl and it was definitely a challenge and competition to get her attention initially.

She was two years younger than I and that didn't bother me at all. However, dating a ninth-grader when someone is in the 11th grade is frowned upon. That still did not stop me from claiming Monique as my girlfriend. My brothers knew Monique from Roselawn Condon and thought she was pretty too. I pursued her persistently and romantically. Monique played hard to get, but she eventually opened up to me and became my girlfriend. Her mother worked for the same fast-food chain as

I did at that time. She worked the hours of three to eleven, so Monique and I had plenty of alone time together.

Her mother, Robyn, liked me as a boyfriend for her daughter. I encouraged Monique for the better and many times I would agree with things her mother would say in regards to Monique. Her mother appreciated the positive support and reinforcement. Monique and I watched weekly television shows and looked forward to quality time with one another. Monique would lay out a cover or we would snuggle on the couch and enjoy the television shows and each other's presence and company. She shared songs with me that were important to her, cooked for me, and took me around her family. I treated her like my princess too, by showering her with attention, love, and affection. I loved every inch of her and did not see any flaws in her. My relationship with Monique was loving and enduring and taught me the true meaning of intimacy and priorities.

Monique let me into her heart and I let her in mine. We had an amazing connection together. She allowed me more access to her body the more comfortable she became with me. I took things at a slow speed that she was comfortable with. Initially, I'm certain Monique believed she was going to wait until marriage to have sex. However, we both were infatuated and found each other irresistible. As our relationship developed, Monique expressed herself physically towards me. She let me know how much she enjoyed my touch with her expressions. We were genuinely in love and our physical contacts continued to escalate with her consent.

During the relationship, Monique grew to adore having new experiences with me. I didn't know tons, but I was equipped enough to give the impression like I had a lot of experience. The truth is I was still learning too. However, because I really cared about Monique, I never would push too hard about us having sex. With time and patience, Monique began to consider giving her virginity to me. I would try to convince her at times, but it did not matter to me how long it was going to take. In my mind, Monique was worth the wait.

Our intimate times started to escalate and advance as Monique was assured of my faithfulness towards her. She allowed me more access to her body as she grew comfortable with me being her boyfriend. We took showers together and washed each other's bodies. I treated her like the princess she was and the excess time we spent together cemented our bond. One day, Monique and I were hanging out at her house and having another intimate moment. We were in her bed naked and I gave attention to her entire body. I carefully investigated each of her reactions and responses to find the spots that brought her the most pleasure. I gave her oral sex that day, and soon after, Monique could resist me no longer. She wanted to have an intimate experience with me, so we made love and it was special for both her and me. We truly had an enduring devotion to one another. Monique and I spent countless hours together building our connection. Although she was younger than I, that did not stop me from claiming her as my girlfriend. Some of the girls on my grade level who were interested in me would voice their disapproval, but it would fall on deaf ears. I was committed and loyal to Monique throughout our relationship.

Monique and I went to prom together during my junior year when Monique was just a freshman. Our relationship lasted well into my senior year. In my senior year, I wanted to spend more time with my friends. This was difficult to do because Monique had grown accustomed to ample access she had to me. Monique would often complain about the time I spent hanging out with friends, rather than spending the time with her. It was cute at first, but Monique was adamant about curbing the time I spent away from her.

Things between us were great until I informed her that I had made the decision to join the Air Force. Monique became worried and rightfully so. She became extremely clingy and emotionally distressed. She did not want me to go away to the military and expressed her concern to me openly. At the time, I did not realize that she was simply concerned about the future of our relationship. She needed me to reassure her that everything would be okay, but I was too young to understand exactly what it was that she needed from me. I took her reaction as doubt or mistrust in my decision. I misinterpreted her emotions and received it like she did not believe in me. The emotional hardships began to put a strain on the relationship. I loved her dearly, but I put some space between us for me to continue to grow as a young man. This only made things worse. One time during an argument and eventual break-up, Monique threatened to harm herself. I got in my car and rushed over to her house to check on her. She had not harmed herself, but she was an emotional wreck and it was the breaking point for our relationship.

Monique was a homebody and an anti-social kind of person. She did not wish to join me really when I went out with my friends. One weekend, my friends and I went to the club Ritz. After the club let out, we were in my car passing through an alleyway adjacent to the parking lot. Some girls were walking by in the alley when one of my friends yelled out to them and they responded back. We stopped the car and began to converse with the girls. I was good looking and good at conversation, so I left with one of their numbers. I had no idea this girl would become my next girlfriend.

After one full day, I called Mary on the phone and tried to get to know her. It was my rule not to call a girl for a day after I got a number. I was taught that it made someone seem desperate if they called too early. Mary was somewhat distant at the beginning, which I found as an interesting challenge. Monique and I were in emotional turmoil following our breakup, so Mary's fun personality provided me a possible escape. The toil of my relationship was overwhelming me emotionally.

After about a week, Mary explained to me why she was being distant towards me. She told me that she was involved with a well-known star basketball player in the city from her school. She admitted to allowing him to perform oral sex on her during one of the times I could not get ahold of her on the phone. Mary stated that she wanted to be honest and it had occurred when we were talking, and not officially dating. I was a bit jealous and angry at first, but I couldn't be mad because I appreciated her telling me the truth. Mary was aware that I still had lingering feelings for Monique and immediately felt threatened by them. Mary became concerned about my commitment towards her, so she set a plan in motion to ward off Monique even further.

Monique was already hurt by the fact that I was moving away and going into the military. The fact that our relationship was coming to an end started to settle in as a reality. I became more distant and detached once Mary came into the picture. Monique began to seek attention from my friends and enemies in an attempt to get back my attention. This only drew me further away from her. Mary took every opportunity to remind me that Monique was betraying me with friends and enemies. Monique tried to salvage our relationship by attending social events where she knew I would be. During a basketball game after school, Monique oddly attended the social event and made it obvious that she wanted me back. However, Mary was present at the game and aggressively marked her territory. Mary sat next to me and scowled at Monique anytime she would look my way.

Mary was a sexy, brown-skinned, sassy bombshell. She was up to date on style and what was current. Mary had sexy confidence in herself and was a bit possessive and aggressive in our relationship. She knew what she wanted and was relentless about pursuing it. Mary was very persuasive about getting her way and would throw a fit if she didn't. However, I found her very attractive and fun because she kept things interesting. She played hard to get and the challenges intrigued me. Mary made me express my feelings for her before doing anything with me physically. She wanted the same loyalty and romancing that I had shown Monique in our relationship. I had become skilled at sweet-talking and charming a girl, but Mary was a player in her own right.

Mary was younger than I, but she was much more sexually advanced in some ways. She was skilled in the acts she performed sexually and it made me feel special for being with her. Mary would often try new things with me and questioned me about the pleasures it gave me. We spent a lot of time together and quickly fell in love with one another. I remember one time when I was at her house and she wanted to have anal sex with me. I was not ready for all that at the time she offered it. I was satisfied with the sensations from the oral and vaginal sex we had. She jokingly called me a punk about the anal, but we made up for it with other endeavors that night.

Mary had great hygiene and was always fresh down below, which led me to accept every invitation she gave me. Mary had a sexual drive and she expected me to fulfill all of her wild fantasies. Looking back, I believe Mary just wanted to be my first in areas that Lynn had overlooked. Being intimate with Mary was a thrilling and thriving experience for me during that time in my life. I would go over to her house on the weekends and we would cuddle and watch movies in her living room. When no one was around, the movie was actually watching us. We would tell her mother we were going to the movie rental store to retrieve some flicks for that evening. We would get movies, but we would pull the car over and have sex on our way back.

The steam produced on the windows provided us with all the cover we needed.

During art class in my senior year, I had learned how to sew and I made Mary a present with our first project. I sewed a doll that resembled her and was made in her likeness for Valentine's Day. She absolutely loved the gift and we referred to it as the "Mary Doll." I learned the impact a thoughtful gift could have and tried to impress Mary every chance I got. She showed interest in my talents and was supportive of my hobbies and interest. Mary never complained about the time I spent with my friends, but instead would invite herself whenever she wanted my time. Mary would often bring along another pretty girl to occupy my friends during that time. My crew benefitted from Mary's tactful accommodation.

Mary's mother adored me! I always had a positive influence on the girls I dated. I encouraged and challenged them to become better people. Mary's mother noticed that good influence and allowed us to spend time together often. One time, my first vehicle's engine had blown and I was out of transportation. This was a major obstacle for me because I was active socially, needed transportation to school, and needed to maintain my part-time job. I had saved up $650 dollars from previous paychecks, but this was not nearly enough to find a car in the public.

I searched newspapers and every resource I had available to me at the time. I then heard about an auction that was being held in a local neighborhood. Mary's mother had learned about the auction as well because she was looking for a vehicle for her older son. We all went to an auction and I was optimistic that my $650 would be enough to purchase a car. Little did I know, cars were being sold left and right for much more money than I came equipped with. My girlfriend's mother had spotted a green car for her son and got the vehicle for him once it was auctioned off. My chances of getting a car dwindled with every car that was sold.

I desperately and patiently watched as people bid in numbers larger than I had in my wallet. I began to become disappointed by the failed attempts to secure some form of transportation. Then came the last car of the auction. It was a blue hatchback Ford Escort. I bid on the vehicle twice, before the auctioneer announced "seven-fifty." I knew my chances were over for leaving the auction with a car. In grief, I looked up at Mary's mother, and in pure confidence, she nodded her head at me. I gazed at her in confusion and looking into my eyes, she nodded again. As I hesitantly raised my hand she nodded again and I understood what she meant. Her nod was a signal for me to continue to bid. I got back in auction at $900 dollars. Others were bidding on the car, but Mary's mom had already sized-up this man I was competing with. She knew exactly when to counter and give me a signal to bid. In joy and excitement, we bought the car for $1100 dollars. I was relieved and ecstatic!

I gathered up the $650 dollars I had saved and Mary's mom provided the additional $450 dollars for me to close the deal. I was shocked that she did this for me, but I assured her and gave my word that I would pay her back every penny. She wasn't worried about the money really, but the mother accepted my repayment promise. I indeed paid her back the $450 dollars in a timely manner with my first military paychecks.

I dated Mary until I joined the Air Force after high school. She was the first girl my Mother allowed to spend the night at my house, the day prior to me leaving for the military. We cuddled each other and talked that night, but we did not have sex. Mary was on her period, but of course Mary taunted me to go forward with it anyway. I was not ready for that experience either, so I merely enjoyed her company and held her close that night. I stayed in the basement for several years and was never once bothered by any kind of insects. The one night she stayed over, a spider came out and jumped on her. Maybe that was a sign of what was to come. The next morning, she came with my family to wish me well as I departed for greener pastures. I remember waving her good-bye as I left Cincinnati by bus headed for the military. We planned to continue our relationship and I vowed to contact her as soon as possible.

I can't talk about the important girls in my life without bringing up Nicole. She was very special to me and played a major part in my life. She was brown-skinned with an athletic build. She had a gap in the front of her teeth, but her smile could light up a room. She wasn't fairest of them all, but she was adorable and attractive to me. Nicole was competitive and active in sports, which I appreciated as an athlete. She was never my girlfriend, but she had access to me at all times regardless of who I was with. I first met her when her older brother dated my sister. We were in elementary at that time we met. Nicole was a year older than my brother and two years younger than I. One time, she rode her bike with a mutual friend, Danielle, to my house. I remember her stopping by because Nicole had a Kool-Aid stain on her shirt. I reminded her of it every now and then and we would laugh about that Kool-Aid stain as we grew older.

I learned that Nicole had an interest in me much more than I was aware of initially. Nicole was confident in who she was and wasn't afraid to go after what she wanted. We had a lot in common, including a similar taste in music, humor, and zodiac sign. She understood me more than any other girl. Nicole paid attention to what I did and what I said, so she always knew how to communicate effectively with me. I had complete trust in Nicole and put my guards down when I was around her. I let her into my emotions and she was content with being there. Nicole was the best at fulfilling my desires because of her attentiveness to me. She could have whatever she wanted from me, but for some reason that never included the title of girl-friend.

Nicole was my bottom chick and an instrumental figure in my childhood years. Nicole could bring out the best in me by understanding my moods and reading my responses. She always added positive energy whenever she was around and admired the person I was. She wasn't concerned with a title be-cause she had access to my heart. She was the second girl I had sex with, but it was like both of our first times. We had sex many other times after that. We had oral sex as well and Nicole knew how to bring my body pleasure like nobody else. Nicole and I had an obvious connection that cemented our bond. I wish I would have taken that chemistry more seriously, but re-gardless we had many great times together. No matter who I was going out with, Nicole was always somewhere nearby.

Aimee was another girl who never was my girlfriend, but we were extremely close. I knew her since kindergarten and she lived right across from me in my neighborhood. Her brother and I were good friends and played outside together often. In elementary school, I never paid much attention to Aimee in re-gards to dating her. We were friends and I had a lot of respect for her family and her religion. Aimee's family were Muslim and I learned tons about their religion just from being associated with them. Her father would come to our school and present the classroom with some of the important facts and history about their practice. This helped us understand Aimee better because she did not participate in any of the holiday activities and she was permitted to sit with her head down during the pledge of allegiance. As kids, we saw Aimee as an African girl, but I never considered her for a girlfriend.

As Aimee grew up, she began to blossom and find her own identity. She was short in stature, but her body soon started to take shape. Aimee was active in activities, smart and ambi-tious in personality. Aimee started to assert and express herself, which drew my interest in her more and more as time went on. We never became boyfriend and girlfriend, but we got much closer than we ever were in grade school. I cared about her, so I did not want to risk the friendship by hurting her feelings in a relationship. I was a young man whose hormones were at full throttle and Aimee demanded a full commitment from me. At the time, I did not want to risk losing her friendship, so we just remained good friends.

Aimee asked me to take her to her prom, and I did, even though my girlfriend Mary was not happy about it. Her family was comfortable with me taking her, and I treated her like the princess she was that night. We danced the night away and stayed in a hotel, but we did not have sex. Aimee was having such a great time partying, and I knew she rarely got an opportunity to freely express herself. I watched over her that evening and safely returned her home the next day. We remained good friends and Aimee did give me an opportunity to sleep with her afterward. However, Aimee demanded my respect, so she made the offer during a time when she knew I would be with my girlfriend. She was forcing me to make a choice. My girlfriend was already upset that I went with her to prom and she was convinced that we did more than I reported to her. At the time, I did want to risk losing my girlfriend, so I didn't show up for Aimee's invitation.

Being raised by women, I never really had any issues with speaking to girls or expressing how I felt. In fact, my upbringing gave me a prowess with dating girls. It was easy for me to talk to the opposite sex and figure out what was important to them. My Mother wasn't extremely affectionate towards me, but she showed her love in many other ways. Needless to say, a part of me craved physical affection. I made several mistakes in dating and in love as many do in their youth. Unfortunately, I have broken a few hearts myself. I can honestly say that I learned something from each and every relationship or experience I had growing up. My hope is that in some way being with me may have made those girls a little bit better in some way as well. I cared for every single girlfriend I had and gave my best effort to remain faithful and be loving.

After getting played by Rachael, I responded by not fully trusting girls as a way to protect my heart from being broken again. I established safeguards, but I still would give my best effort in making my girlfriend happy. It was likely my fault as to why most of my relationships didn't work, but I was young and dumb.

I cherish those youthful and joyful memories that I was fortunate enough to experience. The majority of the girls I dated eventually seemed to do okay after we dated. Some got married later in life, which I took as a sign that they had at least learned how to pick a good guy. I learned something useful about girls or myself from each relationship I had.

I take full responsibility for the mistakes I made in my youth with girls. After my Dad passed away, a part of me felt the need to grow up fast and experience life early, before it was too late. There was peer pressure to have sex, but that does not excuse any of the choices I made. Some of my decisions with girls were wrong, but the love and laughter I shared with them were right. I was always charming, romantic, funny, caring, and thoughtful in my relationships. I was fortunate enough to have many opportunities for relationships at a young age. I made several mistakes, but I learned from each and every one of them. Ultimately, I cared for and respected every girlfriend I ever had because they each taught me something in life or about myself.

"Whoever tries to hide his sins will not succeed, but the one who confesses his sins and leaves them behind will find mercy."
Proverbs 28:13

Illustrated by Davide Dart Rota

Epilogue

I want to walk worthy, my calling to fulfill
Yes, order my steps Lord
And I'll do Your blessed will
The world is ever-changing
But You are still the same
If You order my steps, I'll praise your name

CPSIA information can be obtained
at www.ICGtesting.com
Printed in the USA
LVHW030957100121
676041LV00005B/516